WOODY YAEGER 1998

DECORATIVE SIGNS AND EAGLES
WOODCARVING

CARVING, FINISHING & GOLD LEAFING

by

DAVID HASSELL

TILLER
PUBLISHING
ST. MICHAELS, MARYLAND

DEDICATION

This book is dedicated to the past and the future.
In loving memory of my mother, Pauline, father, Floyd and my brother, Paul.
And in anticipation of a great future for my children: Courtney, Lindsay and Jake,
and my niece and nephew, Becky and Greg.

Acknowledgements

Carol Deakin for her assistance with text and photography. My wife, Lyn, for her many hours
spent taking photographs, typesetting and for just being there. Marion Yablonski for her
proof readng abilities. Jon Wilson of WoodenBoat *for assuring me that I could do this.*
Jeff Goldstein for his encouragement. James Earl Jones for his interest in the raw manuscript
which inspired me to complete the book after it had been lying around for over a year. Skip Allen Sr. of
Southern Boating *for sending the manuscript to Jay Benford and Jay for taking a chance on me.*
Most of all I want to thank all of my clients who ordered signs from me over the past 30 years.
This allowed me to make a living doing work I truly enjoy.

Graphic design and production by: Words & Pictures, Inc., 27 South River Road South, Edgewater, MD 21037.
Cover production by: Palm Tree Studio, Inc., 2529 Cheval Drive, Davidsonville, MD 21035

Photography by: David Hassell, Lyn Hassell, Carol Deakin

Printed in the USA by: Edwards Brothers, Inc., 8401 Corporate Drive, Suite 540, Landover, MD 20785

Questions regarding the content of this book should be addressed to:

TILLER PUBLISHING
P.O. Box 447
St Michaels, MD 21663
410-745-3750 • Fax: 410-745-9743

TABLE OF CONTENTS

INTRODUCTION

I love to carve wood. If you've picked up this book, that probably means you feel the same way. If you see a fine piece of wood and even think about carving something into it, that means there's a woodcarver lurking within. Maybe you haven't taken the time to learn how to carve because you think you don't have the knowledge or experience to do it. Maybe you think the tools are too expensive, a workshop is too hard to create, and you can't afford to take so much time for yourself.

I am going to change your thinking with this book. If you sincerely *want* to carve, you *can*. I've written this book with the untrained woodcarver in mind, but I've also included some more complicated projects for advanced carvers — which is what I want to help you become.

My own life experience should encourage you because I am not a formally trained woodcarver, yet I've managed to support my family with this craft for more than a quarter of a century. This is my sole means of support. I left a career in sales to pursue this work when I was twenty-nine years old, because I needed to do work that was more personally meaningful, less stressful and didn't require driving a hundred miles a day around New York City during the gas crisis of the 1970s.

Luckily, I was able to turn my interest in woodcarving as a hobby into a successful career. This book, though, isn't about how you can make a living as a woodcarver. I am just sharing some of the techniques I've developed as a professional in the hope that you will use them to learn a satisfying hobby.

Woodcarving came into my life when I was eight years old and had the good fortune to live across the street from Wilbur Corwin, one of the leading duck decoy carvers in the world. He was a patient man who didn't mind letting a kid sit and watch him work.

When I was in high school, I did my first carving in art class. It was a mahogany fruit bowl that I made as a gift for my mother. It wasn't very good, but it made me aware that I loved the feel of a chisel against wood. Woodcarving became my passionate hobby. I didn't realize it would become my life's work until that fateful day when I traded my suit and tie for T-shirts and shorts.

I rented a little shop and started doing marine woodcarving, probably because my family has long enjoyed a powerful relationship with boats and the sea. My grandfather and father were always involved with boats. I've had boats since I was a boy on the Great South Bay, but I noticed, as time passed, that I got even more pleasure out of fixing boats than sailing them. It was a natural inclination for me to want to carve things for boats.

In my first shop, I set to work making cockpit grates and carved nameboards in an effort to have something to show and sell at my first boat show in Stamford, Connecticut. It became clear right away that nameboards were my niche because I took orders for about two dozen of them. Nobody really wanted grates. That confirmed my decision to go into marine woodcarving, and it set me to work at a frantic pace to produce high quality nameboards on a real production schedule. Doing one project is a different thing from doing twenty. It required me to hone my skills as both a good and fast craftsman. People were waiting.

Old-school marine woodcarvers may initially resist some of the techniques I've developed, such as the use of power tools along with handtools. Computer generation of lettering templates is my preferred method of getting my patterns. I will also make recommendations for modern finishing systems that have proven their superiority to previous methods. All of these adaptations do nothing to dilute the integrity of the end product, they save time and frustration, and their use can actually make a more beautiful and durable project.

I hope you'll find this book useful and fun. And I hope you'll discover the special pleasure in marine woodcarving that I've enjoyed for such a long time.

Author's note about the focus of this book: I'm concentrating on nameboards and eagles. There is no information about figureheads, billet heads, trailboards and other marine carving of this type. There is virtually no call for this type of work today. Due to space and time constraints for this book, I opted not to cover these subjects. If your interests lie in these areas, I recommend *Shipcarver's Handbook* by Jay Hanna or *Shipcarvers of North America* by M.V. Brewington. You can use these books for design ideas and the techniques for carving them from this book.

CHAPTER 1
GETTING STARTED: SETTING UP A WORKSHOP

It's great to have a fully equipped woodworking shop, but most people don't. My shop is a very functional and comfortable space, but I've been doing this for half of my life. I started carving in a towel on my lap! Obviously, when my work moved from being a hobby to a job, I had to create a real shop.

My shop isn't perfect. I can still get frustrated when I'm handling really large projects and take out a fluorescent bulb or two while turning a long board.

Still, I appreciate my shop. You need to look around your house — or wherever you plan to work — and choose a spot where you can, first, make a mess.

Woodchips and sawdust and finishing products are very messy. Even work on a small project is going to generate a fair amount of chips and dust, and you need to create a space for yourself where you don't have to worry about cleaning up when you're in the middle of carving. When you complete carving and move on to finishing, you will need good ventilation.

The most important consideration of all in setting up a shop or workspace is good lighting. If you can't see it, you can make a lot of costly and frustrating mistakes. I like fluorescent lighting and plenty of it. The work should be lighted from every direction and you should never have a shadow cast over your work by your hands. I also use two or three adjustable lamps at my carving bench.

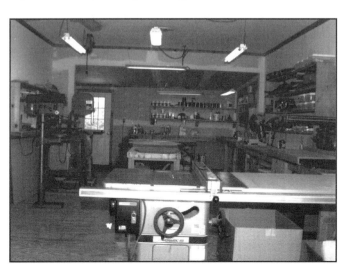

A solid workbench is critical. You don't want your bench walking around as you work. I have a bench design in the projects section of this book if you need to build one. For small projects, buy yourself a non-skid workpad to keep your little jobs from walking away.

I like to sit and carve. It is useful to have a nice, comfortable chair with large wheels. Small wheels can catch on woodchips.

You can't have enough work surfaces. My workshop has a small bench for carving, a larger bench for bigger projects, and a table where I do a lot of finishing processes. I also have a lot of counters and cabinets around the perimeter where I store tools and finishing materials. A word about storing the finishing materials: be careful with them. Secure them if you have small children who are still young enough to get into things. Put a lock on whichever cabinet you use to keep these chemicals away from little hands. One day, water based products will improve enough to withstand the particular demands of the marine environment, but, at this writing, petroleum-based products are still superior. Take care with their storage, use and disposal.

I have a power cord rolled up overhead. You won't believe how handy this is when I'm working at the main bench. I can plug in whichever tool I need right over my work, so I don't have to go far from the bench. It's the same kind of cord that car repair garages have.

There is an exhaust fan installed in an exterior wall and I don't know how I would work without it. It carries away dust and fumes.

Drying racks made from a dowel system on the wall are great to allow work to dry. The exhaust fan draws dust from this area, so I never have to worry about what sanding in one end of the shop is doing to the wet finishes of nameboards lying on the dowels.

The best thing about my shop is that it's far away from the living areas of my house, tucked into the two-car-garage. You may not have this luxury, but you also probably aren't in the business of wood-carving and would just as soon keep your cars in a garage if you have one.

What you need, as I've already said, is a peaceful corner where you can do your work without worrying about the mess. You need a place that doesn't have to be completely cleaned each time you have to stop working for a day or two. If you can't have your tools out ready to resume work, you may not take them out as often as you would like. And you'll never get any carving done.

You don't need all of the equipment I have and you certainly don't need the space if you're only interested in woodcarving as a hobby for a few projects.

So, look around your house or office and see if you can create a corner with a sturdy bench, good lighting, ventilation, a regular power source, and a storage cabinet for your tools and supplies.

CHAPTER 2
THE WOOD

The wood used in marine woodcarving is very special. Teak and mahogany are some of the most beautiful woods in the world and are the traditional woods used in marine application. The reason is that they hold up very well in an environment that is continually wet and generally salty—a demanding situation for wood.

Pine was once the chosen wood of shipcarvers, but it is so soft that it requires extremely sharp tools to carve. Despite its historic application, nobody is putting pine on their boats now. I never use it in my work.

Kiln-dried Burmese teak and genuine mahogany are the woods I prefer to carve. You may not have a source where you live. Fortunately, there are good suppliers of teak and mahogany who will mail-order your materials to you no matter where you are. Several suppliers I have used and recommend are listed in the resources section of this book.

Avoid luan or Phillipine mahoganies because they are inferior woods. Stress to your lumber dealer, whether you are lucky enough to have one nearby or develop a relationship with a supplier somewhere else, that you're doing woodcarving. You aren't building furniture. If you make this clear, your suppliers will scout their stock for good wood suited to your needs.

Wood for carving is uniformly tight in the grain and this makes a big difference. You can spot a piece of good wood by looking at the cut end to examine the grain. Seek wood that has grain nearly perpendicular or on a 25 to 45 angle to the surface plane. Avoid wood where the grain runs at a severe angle or curved to the surface because this promises misery in carving. Eyeball the surface of the wood, too, and be very critical in spotting wavering grain lines that are not parallel to the edges. Knots and worm holes may be a problem on some projects, so buy your wood with a thought about how much may be wasted due to the natural defects.

Even after 25 years of selecting wood, I can still be unpleasantly surprised by hidden defects. I've had whole boards that looked beautiful and turned out to be terrible disappointments. What you have to remember is that this is a natural product. That's partly the joy of it. It's also partly the frustration. Just make your best selection, adapt to the natural imperfections, and work with it.

Woodcarving is a very labor intensive effort. It has been my experience that the cost difference between good and poor wood is nearly negligible once the project is finished. The difference between a satisfying and unsatisfying project, though, can make the difference in whether you want to continue to carve or not.

Good grain shown on the bottom and bad grain on the top in both photo and drawing.

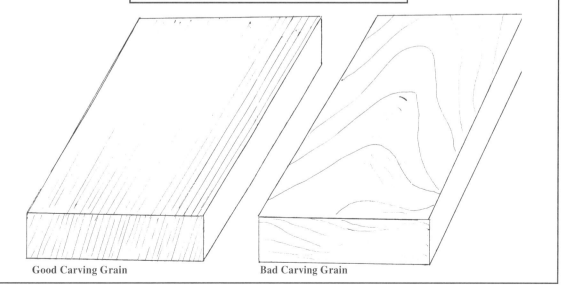

Good Carving Grain   Bad Carving Grain

CHAPTER 3
LETTERING

I work in an old craft using some modern techniques. Just as modern carving techniques can be paired with traditional methods for a better end product, so can modern methods of lettering.

I'll tell you right away that I don't hand letter my patterns. I used to do it that way, but that was before the age of high speed computer technology. I would spend considerable time laboring over my lettering and that wasn't really what I wanted to be doing. I wanted to be carving.

Pure traditionalists will insist upon hand lettering the old way and that's alright. If you have the time, patience and discipline and don't mind devoting years to learning how to hand letter well, this may be important to you. Hand lettering is an art form for which I don't have the time with orders waiting to be done.

There are several inexpensive programs available for your PC that you can use to make your layouts. My preference is to go down to your local sign shop with your design, dimensions and choice of typeface in mind. For a very minimal fee, the professionals there turn out a pattern in a short amount of time. I get a pattern ready in minutes instead of the hours I used to spend hand lettering.

Since I'm a regular customer — and since I live in a coastal community where signage for boats is a common project for these businesses — the owner is accustomed to addressing my needs. I get invited to the back room to stand over the computer operator and give directions while he or she plugs in the information. You will find it helpful to develop this kind of relationship with a signmaker because it saves a lot of time, money and aggravation. The more accustomed they become to working to your specifications, the easier it will be to get the pattern you need the first time you ask for it.

If my nameboard blank is small enough to carry, I'm likely to take it right down to the signmaker's shop. Especially when I'm dealing with something less straightforward, such as a name with a curved baseline, the computer's mathematical accuracy eliminates the visual deceptions that can make hand lettering go awry.

One big advantage of computer generated lettering is that computer programs dealing with letters are based on traditional type design. The computer already knows, for example, that the letters "S" and "O" are among a small group of letters which are a bit taller in proportion to most of the other letters in a given font. The subtlety of the height difference is not apparent until you examine it closely. When you are hand lettering, you may miss this nuance altogether until it's too late and the board is carved.

I think it bears mentioning that the explosion in computer software among competing companies has made things a little confusing in terms of typeface names. The same typeface may carry an altogether different name in two different programs. There's no reason for it, but the situation exists and I just want you to be aware of it.

You'll need relatively few typefaces for marine woodcarving. These can be found in the *Gerber Catalog of Designs and Numbers*, a reference book only available at your signmaker's shop.

TYPEFACES OR FONTS FOR MARINE WOODCARVING

In general terms, typefaces come in 3 styles: serif, sans serif and script. Serif faces are distinguished by what I call little tails at the top and bottom. Sans serif are without this ornamentation.

Some of the typefaces I use are:

Serif:

TIMES BOLD	**Times Bold**
TIMES NEW ROMAN	Times New Roman
UNIVERSITY ROMAN	University Roman
PEGASUS	**Pegasus**
TIFFANY MEDIUM	Tiffany Medium
CENTURY	Century

Script:
Commercial
Cotillion

Sans Serif:

HELVETICA	Helvetica
UNIVERS	Univers
MODERNE	Moderne

In general, the serif types are ideally suited to traditional marine woodcarving. They may be modernized by slanting them to the right. The sans serif without stylistic embellishments — tails —are more suited to sleek, modern craft. When these are slanted to the right, they give an even more streamlined effect that is very much at home on futuristic power boats.

A note on serifs: I use the Times Bold style more often than any other. (My customers request it.) This letter style, when drawn by the computer, has blunted points. This makes carving difficult and really isn't necessary, so I usually just take the serif to a sharp point as shown in the photo.

LETTER HEIGHT

As far as the size of your letters, I strongly recommend staying within a range of from 2 to 4 inches in height when you are learning to carve. Smaller letters require a lot of experience to do well because the carving can be like micro-surgery at moments. You may become frustrated with a lot of delicate cuts.

Very large letters will demand steadiness and perfection beyond the ability of most new carvers. Any variation in the straightness of a line becomes uncomfortably apparent in a long run. Large letters also invite any defect in the wood grain to make itself known.

CHAPTER 4
THE TOOLS

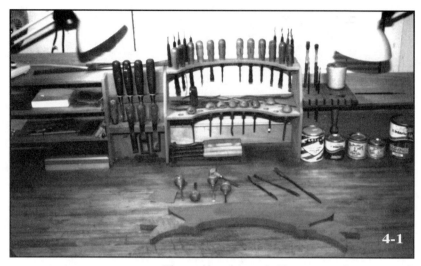

The workbench is probably your most important tool. You can see that the one I use has a place for everything. It's very helpful to be organized. There is a drawing for a simple bench in the plans and patterns section.

Now that you've created a good place to do your woodcarving, it's time to build your inventory of tools. I recommend a combination of hand and power tools. There are some woodcarvers who use hand tools exclusively and would never consider using power.

If you have all the time in the world, you can shun power. I find them to be invaluable workhorses in my tool arsenal because they MOVE wood in minutes that would take hours or days to do by hand. I regard them as useful, modern technology applied to an ancient craft. I think the application works very well.

Hand-held power tools, such as routers, drills, sabre saws, a beltsander, orbital and random action sanders and an angle grinder used in conjunction with sanding disks are relatively inexpensive power tools any serious hobbyist should buy.

Stationary power tools, such as a table saw, band saw, drill press, radial arm saw, joiner, thickness planer and scroll saw are some of the much larger equipment I use regularly. Now, these may be expensive to buy and aren't tools you can store in a cabinet. Most people don't have the space or inclination to invest in these tools.

Fortunately, you can get your boards prepared by a professional woodworker if you take your dimensions and boards to a local shop. If you have a neighbor with these tools and the skill to use them, you can surely work out an arrangement of some kind. The point is, don't be intimidated by the idea you have to go out and buy a lot of heavy duty equipment. You aren't going to be building furniture. You're going to be a woodcarver.

Hand tools are the soul of the carving experience. When the loud machines are off, the dust settles and you set to work with your hand moving the tools into the grain of the wood, you're into the best part of the experience.

Hand tools come in both short and long-handled types. Traditionalists favor long-handled tools because there are several advantages. The quality of the longer tools is generally better, there is tremendous variety in more than two hundred shapes and sizes, and longer tools are used in the standing position — regarded as the traditional posture.

I haven't found myself attracted to long-handled tools because I enjoy being closer to my carving.

I like to sit when I'm carving and always have, so the shorter tools are the most appealing to me. I haven't been especially motivated to change my ways.

Something else appealing about shorter hand tools is that they're considerably less expensive, as well as easier to use.

Getting down to purely practical matters for beginners — or even the moderately experienced woodcarver — I'm going to recommend a starter set of tools for your shop in the following pages. You'll want to expand upon this list as your interest and abilities increase, but you can get comfortably started if you stock your tool chest with these items.

Woodcraft is one of the best sources for these tools, as well as a mind-boggling array of tools and products specifically geared to the work of the woodcarver. You're going to discover that I make specific product recommendation, but let me say up front: I'm not receiving any endorsements to mention the tools and materials I recommend in this book.

Woodcraft has been offering quality tools for most of this century. Get yourself a catalog — I've included their phone and address in the resources section at the back of this book — and you may give them a call to ask for a catalog. You may be lucky enough to have a good local supplier, and some of the tools can certainly be found at the corner hardware store, but you're going to be very happy if you get to know Woodcraft.

CHISELS

If you plan to follow the carving techniques described in this book, you'll need a grand total of three butt chisels.

I have found that the 1/2", 3/4", and 1¼" bench chisels you can buy at your local neighborhood hardware store will work very well for most carving situations after some modification to them.

These chisels will measure about 7¾" in overall length when you purchase them. You'll want to modify them, so

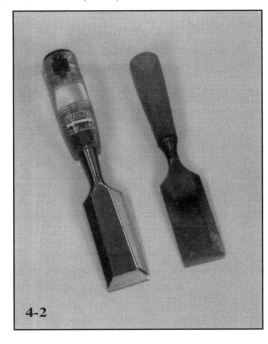

4-2

buy the kind with high impact plastic handles. Cut about an inch off the top of the handle and work the remaining stub into a smaller diameter by turning it against a running belt sander. This alteration gives the chisels superior balance and makes them fit comfortably into the palm of your hand.

If you decide to purchase a ready-made set of stubby carving tools, a 1/2" carving chisel is included and this is a good substitute for the 1/2" plastic-handled chisel.

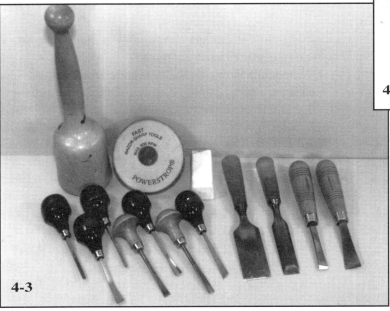

4-3

The minimum set of tools you will need to carve nameboards.

The minimum set of tools you will need to carve nameboards includes (*photo 4-3*):

1. General tools: Carving set no. 1293 (5/16" Bent Gouge, 5/32" Small gouge, 5/32" Bent V Parting Tool, 5/16" Straight Skew, Chisel and 5/16" Bent Square Chisel - this tool is the reason you have to purchase the set).
2. 1¼" and 3/4" Modified Butt Chisels.
3. Mallet
4. Power Strop and Rouge
5. Stubby 1/2" Chisel
6. Stubby 3/4" #3 Gouge
7. Swiss 8mm #5 Palm Handled Gouge
8. Swiss 8mm Palm Handled Chisel

PALM-HANDLED CARVING TOOLS

Woodcraft has a nice variety of Swiss-made, palm-handled tools. You will enjoy a starter set that includes the tools that I use for the majority of my carving *(photo 4-4)*. (There is a complete list with catalog numbers in the Resource section at the back of this book.)

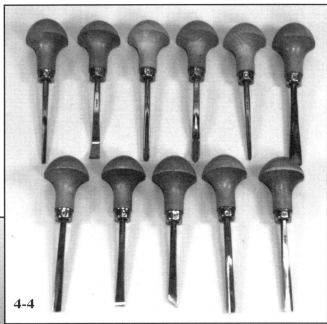

4-4

Perhaps the most important palm-handled tool is the 5/16" bent chisel *(photo 4-5)* from Woodcraft's less expensive set. (The 8mm bent chisel from the most expensive Swiss set is not suitable.) A very useful feature of the palm-handled tools is that the handles are flat on one side, so they're not going to roll off your bench.

The best palm-handled bent chisel is only available from General Tools Mfg. Company. It is in their six piece carving set #1293. Most hardware stores can order this set for you. I use this bent chisel on all the projects in this book.

4-5

MICRO-CARVING SET

Difficult detail cuts require these tiny, extremely sharp hand tools. Available in a full assortment of shapes and configurations, you'll enjoy having these tools to make your way through intricate carving steps. They come pre-honed and you need to be careful not to cut yourself with them. I recommend the micro gouge and dogleg chisel set (photo 4-6) because they work well in almost any situation.

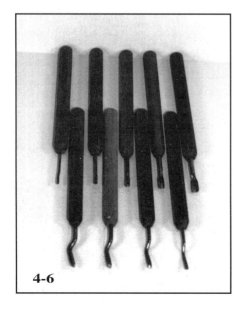

4-6

RIFFLERS

Rifflers come in a wide variety of shapes and sizes and are available in file and rasp cuts (photo 4-7). They are used to remove cut marks from wood in preparation for final sanding, but you'll discover a lot of opportunities to use them during carving. These are shaping tools. Available in tapers, flats, triangles, squares, ovals and more, you will just have to choose your favorite rifflers according to what you like.

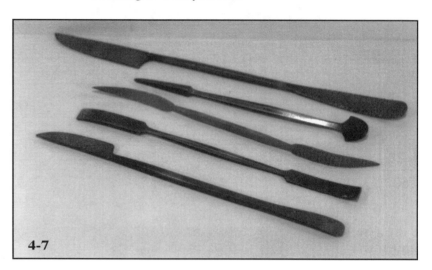

4-7

I have some old Italian rifflers I love, but you aren't going to find these styles for sale new. You might stumble across them at a yardsale, but they just aren't manufactured anymore. Riffler makers are a curious and independent lot — especially the Europeans — and it's hard to understand why they refuse to continue making what I consider to be some of their best designs. The Japanese make respectable rifflers, although I am too content with my old ones to make a serious investigation of them. Since you are starting out, you'll discover new rifflers that work comfortably for you. I advise you to experiment.

A NOTE ABOUT SHARPENING YOUR TOOLS

No matter how sharp your tools are when they're new, they're not going to bring you much pleasure if you don't maintain them. Your hand tools may come to you razor-sharp from your supplier and you will delight in how easily they cut into the wood. When you use them, though, they're going to get dull. When this happens, your interest in carving will suffer because it will be frustrating work.

You can hone them yourself with a leather power strop. This leather disk fits right into your handheld power drill. After using sharpening stones to remove scratch marks, lay a tool blade against the rotating strop coated with an abrasive compound. Sharpening stones come in a variety of shapes and grades. Consult the Woodcraft catalog for recommendations.

You can also send them off to Woodcraft for sharpening. They have an excellent shop that I use when my tools need to be re-ground.

THE MALLET

To tell the truth, I had a change of opinion about mallets as I was writing this book. I've had the same lignum vitae mallet — somewhat modified — for more than 25 years. It was pretty beaten up, but that didn't bother me because it had come to be an extension of my hand. I loved the weight and balance of it.

Then, I got a Brienz carving mallet from Woodcraft. The 8½ oz., one-piece mallet turned from beech has exceptional balance (photo 4-8). My old mallet is now retired, but certainly not forgotten. The Brienz is now my regular tool.

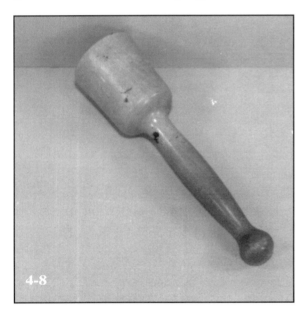

4-8

STORING YOUR HAND TOOLS

An organized workspace is an important part of making woodcarving pleasurable. There is nothing more frustrating than searching in a pile of tools for the right one. When wood chips cover your bench and your tools, your going to get annoyed looking for just the right one.

One of the best organizers I know is a tool rack that holds all your hand tools, including your mallet (photo 4-9). You can't buy one, but you can easily make

one. I'm going to give you a pattern in the projects chapter of this book. In fact, you may want to make this your first project because it will easily introduce you to working with wood in preparation for learning to carve.

POWER SAWS: WHAT THEY DO

This tremendously powerful tool is a stationary table saw with an adjustable, circular blade (photo 4-10). It takes up a lot of space, but it makes easy work of preparing the edges of a nameboard blank.

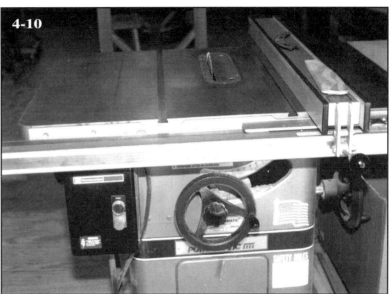

4-10

POWER MITRE BOX AND RADIAL ARM SAW

Both powerful tools, they are adjustable through 180 degrees of angles and are best used for cutting square or angled cuts for the ends of nameboard blanks. (See photos 4-11 and 4-12 on next page.)

4-9

4-11

SABRE SAW

This is the saw most beginners will most likely use because it is inexpensive and can be put away in a cabinet or drawer when it isn't being used. It is ideal for cutting out patterns. A wide assortment of blades gives it great flexibility in terms of projects. If you can afford a good one, I recommend the Porter Cable saw I use *(photo 4-13)*.

4-12

BAND SAW

This stationary saw is tremendously flexible with its ability to use many different width blades to adjust for cutting various radii. It is ideal for cutting out patterns and doing fine work.

SCROLL SAW

Even finer work is available with this remarkable saw. I like using it for very small, fine work where flexibility is of tremendous value. *(See photo 4-14 on the next page.)*

4-13

Upper left, power mitre saw; center left, radial arm saw; and sabre saw, below right.

4-14

Above: the band saw is in the rear, the drill press in the foreground and the scroll saw in between. Below: routers and bits.

OTHER POWER TOOLS

DRILL PRESS

This quiet, stationary tool is ideal for creating bungs or plugs. If you're like me and can't drill a perpendicular hole with a hand drill, it's a must.

ROUTER AND ROUTER BITS

There are a lot of routers on the market. Routers are used for many applications. They use a center rotating bit that cuts away wood on the edge or at the center of a board. If you can only have one router, I recommend the Black and Decker router with two handles that has a light built in *(photo 4-15)*. There are also routers that are ideal for rounding over the edge of projects *(photo 4-16)*. A good assortment of carbide bits is shown in the photo *(photo 4-17)*. They include roundover, cove, chamfer and mortising bits.

4-15

4-16

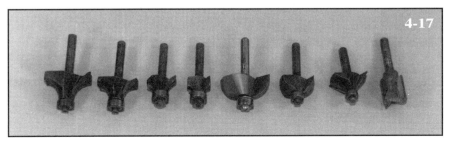

4-17

PLATE (BISCUIT) JOINER AND DOWLING JIG

When you want to edge join two or more pieces of wood, these tools make easy work of it *(photo 4-18)*.

4-18

4-19

ELECTRIC HAND DRILL

You'll use this tool for so many things. Whether screwing or unscrewing projects or drilling holes using all kinds of bits, this inexpensive piece of power equipment is tremendously useful in the woodcarvers shop *(photo 4-19)*.

THICKNESS PLANER

There is probably no power tool noisier than this one. It makes short work, though, of establishing an even plane on a board and smoothing the surface of your wood or attaining the proper thickness prior to sanding. Wear ear protection when you use it. *(See section on pre-curved nameboards for photo of planer.)*

HVLP PAINT SPRAYER (HIGH VOLUME LOW PRESSURE)

This turbine sprayer produces an excellent finish on carved projects with little overspray and the moisture problems associated with all air compressors and traditional spray guns.*(See chapter on finishing for photo of sprayer.)*

SANDERS

There are many different kinds of sanders you can use in woodcarving *(photos 4-20 through 4-23)*. I use beltsanders, random orbit sanders and vibrating sanders. Get yourself one good beltsander and a 1/4 sheet vibrating sander as starter tools, and lay in a good supply of sandpaper.

ANGLE GRINDER, HAND HELD

This is an excellent tool for removing large amounts of wood when roughing out the wings of an eagle.

Are there more tools than these I've mentioned? Of course there are. But these are the ones I regularly use in my shop. I don't expect you to invest in all of these. I just want you to be familiar with the uses of them. If you go on from being a hobbyist to a professional — or at least a very serious hobbyist — you'll need to know about these power tools.

On the non-power side, I also recommend that you get an assortment of C-clamps, a non-skid pad to put on your work bench for doing smaller work, a bench vise to hold your work, a dust brush, a pair of safety goggles and a respirator for use when sanding and varnishing.

4-20

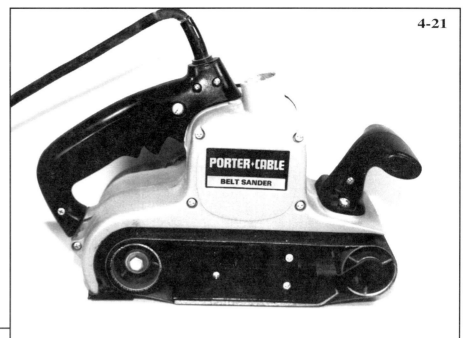

4-21

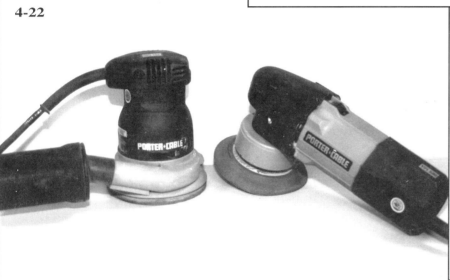

4-22

4-23

CHAPTER 5
HANDCARVING: AN IMPORTANT EXERCISE IN PREPARATION FOR WOODCARVING

This chapter is the most important one in the whole book. That's because handcarving letters involves virtually every carving technique you will ever use as a *bas relief* (pronounced bah) woodcarver.

Bas relief is a term that describes working in three dimensions when the depth of the work is relatively shallow compared to height and width. You are sculpting with wood in a way that makes figures project from the background and it suggests much greater depth than is actually there. If you're working on a nameboard, your board will usually be less than an inch thick.

Bas relief applies to carving eagles, shields and all kind of decorative work, but it is also at the heart of carving letters. In fact, when you learn to carve letters, you are well on your way to being able to carve anything.

Letters are precise geometric shapes that will require you to conform to their specifications. You can apply more of your own creativity — and be able to make more mistakes — when you're carving an eagle or a nameboard blank. Letters, despite the fact that they come in thousands of different typefaces — or fonts as they are known among typesetters — don't allow room for personal style or errors.

Even the untrained eye will be able to tell immediately if a letter hasn't been formed with the right dimensions and proportions. If you've ever driven down a country road and noticed a vegetable stand with crudely lettered sign — upper and lower case randomly mixed — you immediately drew some negative conclusions about the skill level of the signmaker. It's the same conclusion your carved letters will create if you stray from the very precise measurements and dimensions of your chosen typeface.

Before we get into handcarving letters, I'd like for you to do an exercise using basic shapes. Actually, this exercise is so valuable in helping an aspiring woodcarver learn the craft that you could spend the next six months doing it over and over until you know it intuitively.

Consider this your theory work. Just as experienced musicians play the same scales repeatedly to improve his or her performance of music, this exercise is something you should do often because it will make all of your project carving much better.

I developed this exercise somewhere along the line years ago. No matter how often I have done it for demonstration purposes for students, I am always discovering something new it can teach me. Even in the middle of writing this book, I did the exercise twice in a row to be sure I could accurately describe the technique. Not wanting to get up from my bench to find a new scrap, I just turned the first one over. While I had the same symbols to carve, I was confronting the grain going in the opposite direction. I had to adjust my carving style to account for it.

It was a valuable lesson in the grain changes and differences you will find in the same piece of wood. How critical is it to select the correct side of the board for more comfortable carving? I can't tell you — nobody can — which side of the board is going to be more cooperative. Even the best trained professional can't look at a board and know on sight which side is going to be best, except for obvious defects.

If you wanted to improve the odds that you're selecting the best side for your carving comfort, you could buy a long board and cut off the end for experimentation. But let's be realistic: you and I aren't going to do this. We adjust with each project, taking each piece of wood with its own unique merits and flaws, and learn to carve it.

Since this is your first time doing this exercise, I'm going to ask you to do it exactly as I say. After you've done it my way a few times, feel free to adjust my techniques and choice of tools to suit your own way of working. No matter if you're a beginner or an experienced woodcarver, try it this way before you develop your own style.

AN EXERCISE WITH 4 SYMBOLS

MATERIALS AND SUPPLIES:

1¼" modified butt chisel	5/8" bent chisel
1/2" stubby carver's chisel	skew
Swiss #5 gouge	mallet
pencil compass	triangle
T-square	straight edge
non-skid pad	

Take a scrap of 7/8" mahogany approximately 4½"x18" and draw the four symbols on the wood as illustrated in the photograph below *(photo H-1)*.

A. Across the grain   B. Angle to the grain

C. With the grain   D. All direction

These symbols will be 2½" in height and 5/8" in width. Using a ruler or straight edge, measure down 1" from the top of the board at two points and draw a line with a pencil all the way across the board.

Measure down 2½" from that line and do another parallel line at he bottom edge of the board.

These two parallel lines determine the height of your symbols.

DRAWING THE EXERCISE SYMBOLS

SYMBOL 1:

Using a T-square or triangle, close the top and bottom lines on the board with two parallel vertical lines placed 5/8" apart.

SYMBOL 2:

Using a triangle, draw two parallel lines angled at 45 degrees, also 5/8" apart.

SYMBOL 3:

Using a T-square or triangle, maintain the same dimensions as Symbol 1 in a horizontal format.

SYMBOL 4:

Using a ruler, find the center point between the two parallel lines on the board and mark it. Put your compass point on this mark and draw a circle that extends just slightly beyond the parallel lines. Measure inward 5/8", adjust your compass, and draw an inner circle from the same center point.

As long as you've done one side, you might as well flip the board over draw the symbols in the same order on the back. It's good to get into the work habit of doing all of the same things in a linear way, especially the dull parts.

CARVING THE SYMBOLS

Working from left to right, you're going to progress from the easiest to the most difficult carving situations. You'll learn to recognize the special features and requirements of each one. These shapes all exist within every letter you will ever carve and most letters will have at least three of these carving situations within them.

SYMBOL 1: ACROSS THE GRAIN

1. Sit down and get comfortable with all your hand tools in an easy reach. Take your 1¼" butt chisel and hold it at a 90 degree angle to the board on the center line at its intersection with the split stops. These are called split stops because they keep you from splitting the wood beyond them. Tap down with your mallet on the chisel just enough to break the surface of the wood. Pick up your chisel and move it toward the other intersection until the entire center line wood surface is neatly broken *(photo H-2)*.

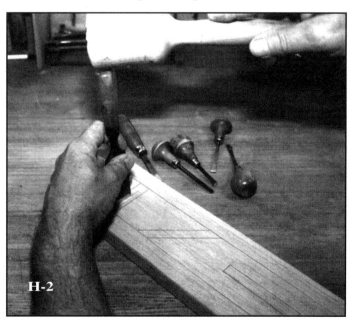

2. Pick up your stubby 1/2" carver's chisel and set the edge of the blade closest to you on one of the split stop lines where it intersects with the center line. Hold it at a 90 degree angle to the board and hit the chisel with your mallet so that you are tapping slightly deeper on the edge of the blade that is right on the intersection. You need the chisel to be buried slightly at the center line and to barely touch the surface of the wood at the other end of the split stop *(photo H-3)*.

H-3

3. Next, hold your 1¼" butt chisel at about a 40 to 45 degree angle to the surface of the wood on the outside right line of the shape. Check your angle and tap the end of the chisel a couple of times with your mallet. These taps should be moderate toward light on impact. You should not be in a hurry to move wood. You're trying to establish your center line plane deep in the board by working gently toward it *(photo H-4)*.

Pull the chisel out and reposition it for the next part of this line by placing the edge of the chisel in the first cut as a reference. You will rock it into position, taking care to observe that you are placing the blade exactly on the penciled line. Place the chisel at the same angle and

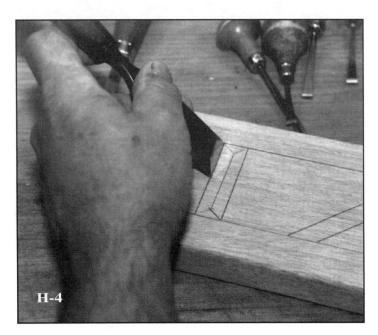

H-4

use the mallet to tap again in the same way. Stay clear of the split stop intersections for now.

4. Now, flip the board around — not over — and do the same steps on the opposite line. Work thoughtfully and carefully, repeatedly flipping the board, maintaining your angle consistently, until you begin to see your center line emerging below the board's surface. Flip the board back and forth, continuing to tap the chisel along the line until you see a clean line in the bottom of the V-shaped trough *(photos H-5, H-6)*.

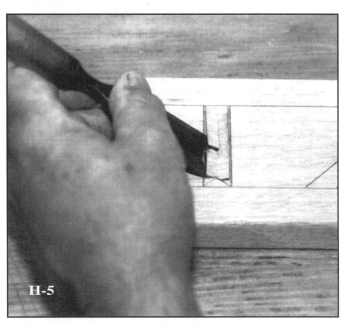

H-5

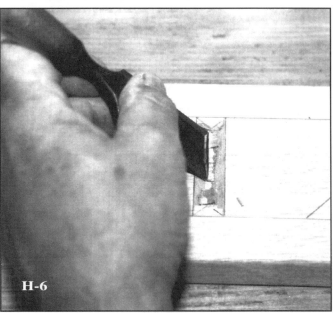

H-6

5. Now it's time to deal with the horizontal lines and the triangular-shaped planes that will descend to meet the center lines at the same 45 degree angle in a very crisp point a the bottom of the trough. Take your bent chisel in hand and, holding it firmly, cut from the top corner to the

Keep using the bent chisel to slice uniform layers away, down to the intersection point. After a while, the triangular plane will reveal itself and its association with the two adjacent vertical planes. You will simply continue to carve until these plane lines become sharp and straight. Look for two very straight, clean, short lines descending at a 45 degree angle from the surface of the wood into the trough.

To repeat these steps on the other horizontal line, flip the board to put it in the same position *(photos H-8 and H-9)*.

intersection point. Repeat from the other top corner. You should rock your bent chisel toward the intersection, bearing in mind that you are maintaining your angle from the outside to the intersection point *(photo H-7)*.

6. Then, go to your top horizontal line and gently slice along it with the bent chisel. Be delicate with this step because you need to determine which way the grain runs. If it fights you and makes little splitting sounds, you're working against the grain and the wood is likely to split outside of your penciled line. In this case, either cut from the other direction or flip the board around until you can slice this line without resistance.

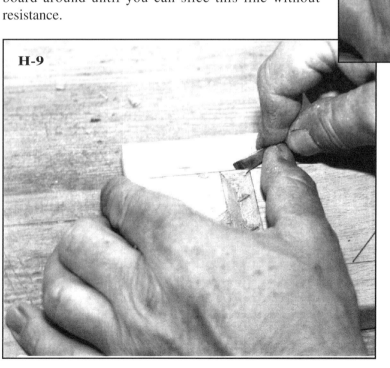

7. Symbol 1 is carved, but it isn't as neat as it should be. Cast a very critical eye to it, clean the obvious problems — lumps in the planes, wavering lines — with your riffler smooth all four planes. Especially for new carvers, these planes will tend to bow at the middle. Get your nose down to the board and really look at those planes. Also, look for areas where your chisel may have grabbed some wood. That happens sometimes because of the wood grain, but it can be minimized with sharp tools. As a final step, fold a piece of 80 grit sandpaper into a square and sand the planes smooth. *(See photo H-10, page 22)*

H-10

SYMBOL 2: ANGLE TO THE GRAIN

At first glance, this exercise in working angle to the grain seems similar to the first one. It is the same shape with a 45 degree slant. Well, that slant makes all the difference. While much of the carving technique is the same, you should follow the same procedure you used in Symbol 1 with some exceptions.

The split stops are different lengths. Where they meet the horizontal line use your skew to make these surface cuts in the shortest lines. When you tap with your mallet, remember to sink the skew deeper at the intersection point of the lines at both top and bottom of the symbol.

Probably the most important tip I can give you with this symbol is: be much less aggressive than you were in the first because splitting can occur at the edges of your chisel. The closer you get to running parallel to the grain, the greater the possibility of splitting the wood. You will have less control over splitting when you are working away from yourself, so try to carve toward yourself whenever possible. Just review the photos and carve the symbol. Remember it's basically the same as Symbol 1 *(photos H-11 and H-12)*.

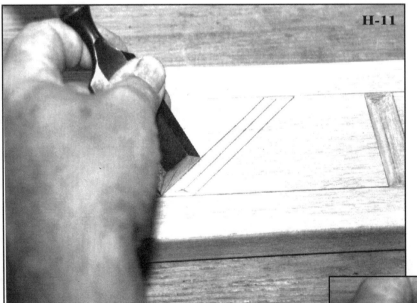

H-11

H-12

SYMBOL 3: WITH THE GRAIN

Draw the center line and split stops as before. If this seems just like Symbol 1, it nearly is. You have returned to 90 degree angles. Before you heave a sigh of relief, the single factor of this symbol being carved with the grain — at a direction rotated 90 degrees from Symbol 1 — is going to surprise you with its complexity.

You will find yourself losing control of the long horizontal lines if you don't take particular care to be ever alert for the sound and feel of runaway grain. The best analogy I can think of is to compare it to boating with or across the current. If you've ever piloted even a jonboat, you know that you have less control when your vessel is parallel to the current in a narrow channel. Slippage can occur before you know it. The same phenomenon applies to entering another boat's wake. Experienced skippers will angle their bow toward a wake to control the rocking motion set up by it; inexperienced ones will take it on the beam with unpleasant rolling from side to side.

Since you're working with the grain, you are parallel to the current of the wood. To keep from slipping off your line, pay keen attention to changes in the grain's movement, and flip your board around as often as you feel you need to in order to maintain control.

Before you carve the two horizontal lines, turn your attention to the short vertical lines that make up the triangular-shaped planes at each end of the trough. With the bent chisel held tightly, slice to define the outside line and cut downward to meet the center line plane at he same 40 to 45 degree angle. As you know by now, you are in patient search of those clean lines where the four planes join together *(photo H-13).*

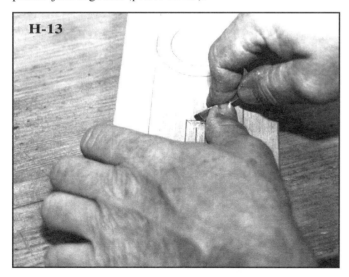

H-13

Break your center line and split stops as usual with a mallet and chisel. Then, put the mallet away. Take your bent chisel — very sharp! —and slice down the center line from one side, staying 3/8" clear of the split stop intersections and maintaining a 40 to 45 degree angle with your chisel. Hold the chisel very tightly. After one

pass down the center line, flip the board and make a similar pass down the other side of the line. You will soon create a ragged mess as illustrated here *(photos H-14 and H-15).*

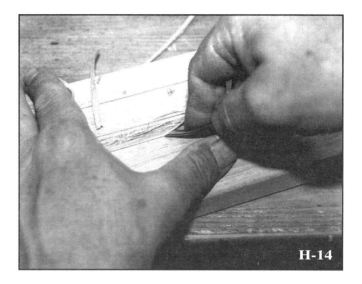

H-14

Avoid a tendency to carve too deeply. (Remember: You can take wood off, but you can't put it back on!) Your ragged mess will evolve into an identifiable center line as you make each pass down the line.

Each pass will back you up to the outside horizontal lines. When you approach this line, be very wary of splits beyond it. If you split outside of it, you've ruined your work. Mistakes within the carving of an actual project can be corrected with filler and covered with gold leaf, but mistakes that split onto the face of the board outside of the carving are nearly impossible to hide.

As you slice carefully along the outside lines, you'll begin to work toward the center line. Keep the angle consistent and the center line will eventually define itself. When you see it, slice it cleanly with your bent chisel and look for two clean planes that descend evenly together. Finish with a Riffler and a folded square of 80 grit sandpaper.

H-15

SYMBOL 4: ALL GRAIN DIRECTION: THE CIRCLE

I've saved the best for last. You've no doubt noticed how each symbol posed more of a challenge than the previous one. This last symbol will combine all the knowledge you've acquired in the first three — and then some.

This is a circle. It is not an "O" with the exception of Helvetica type. This is a circle because the dimension is uniform all the way around.

Take your skew held at a 90 degree angle and break the center line with a mallet. Make your way around the circle in quarters until all four quadrants are connected by this broken surface.

With your bent chisel, grab the edges of the inside radius at the bottom of the circle and slice toward the center line. Remember to maintain your 40 to 45 degree angle. Think of the circle as a clock to keep the quadrants identified. Starting at 6, move clockwise toward 9, rocking and slicing your way around the radius.

For your second quadrant, start at 12 and move counter-clockwise toward 9. You may want to flip the board to make yourself comfortable. Do the same from 12 to 3 and 6 to 3. You may need to change hand position through each quadrant (*photo H-16)*.

Let's talk about split points. By beginning at the points (6 and 12), you are exerting more control by beginning at them, instead of ending at them. The split points are those treacherous areas where the wood is the most likely to take off in following the grain. If you began at 3 and sliced around the quadrant to 12, you are turning from the controlled method of working across the grain to working with or against it. You have much greater control against splitting if you begin your quadrant at these split points. If anything begins to split — you can hear it before you see it — just stop and reverse direction.

You've made a single pass through all four quadrants of the inner plane. You are establishing your center line from the center radius of this symbol because it is a much more controllable approach. Make several more passes in the same order as the first until your bent chisel is backed up to the outside line (the inside radius) where you will carefully slice along it towards the center line.

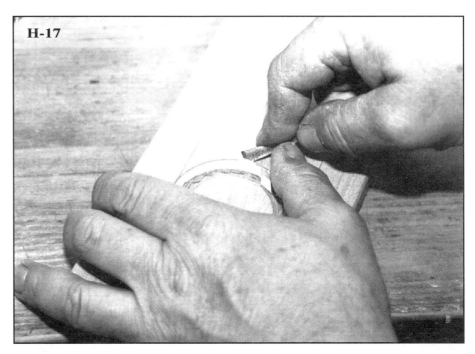

H-17

Scribe the outside radius with your bent chisel just enough to break the surface *(photo H-17 above)*.

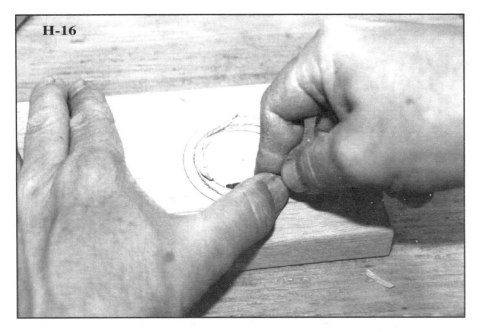

H-16

Take the #5 gouge and slice from the outside radius toward the center line in order to remove wood, maintaining your 40 to 45 degree angle through each quadrant. Try to be consistent in how you use the gouge, rocking it carefully forward. Be very patient. This is difficult carving. If you make sure not to bury both edges of the gouge in the wood, you'll maintain tremendous control against splitting. Keep one edge visible at all times (*photo H-18*).

H-18

When you've made several passes with the gouge, take your bent chisel, lay it right on the outside radius and slice toward you maintaining your angle. Use the thumb of your other hand to guide and push the blade along. You'll begin to notice some fatigue in your muscles because this is hard work. You are concentrating tremendous force in a small point, holding back as much as you are pushing forward. Take a break if you get tired (*photo H-19*).

Take the #5 gouge in hand again and work all the way around the symbol from both sides of the center line. Slice to reduce the "hills" and "valleys" created naturally by this tool. When you have two reasonably smooth planes converging, take the bent chisel and cleanly establish your bottom line. Smooth the planes by using a flat to spoon-shaped riffler. Clean it up with your square of 80 grit sandpaper. You should have a beautiful circle with two smooth planes descending at the same angle to meet in a sharp center line. Now sit back and look at the great job you've done, but not for long (*photos H-20 through H-23 on pages 26 and 27*).

CARVE IT ALL AGAIN

You should be proud of yourself for completing this exercise. It probably seems that you can skip doing it on the back of the board — we're all anxious to get on with real projects we can display — but it is very important for you to do this exercise again.

Flip the board over to the second set of symbols and discover everything you did on the first side is going to be done a bit differently on the back of the board. The procedure and the tools are the same, but the change in carving direction is going to reveal some new challenges.

Much of your carving in terms of hand and board position may be opposite from the first half of this exercise. This is a valuable learning experience. I introduced you to the first side; now, you're going to introduce yourself to this side.

H-19

CHAPTER 6

NAMEBOARDS

Nameboards are the most widely used carved marine decoration in contemporary times. Although there's not much call for trailboards that are specifically built to decorate vintage vessels, modern yachts readily accept the added beauty of a handsome nameboard on the transom or each side. In a boating scene increasingly dominated by painted or vinyl lettering, a carved teak or mahogany board with gold leaf is a standout that emphasizes the owner's commitment to his or her boat.

A nameboard should be designed with careful thought to the style and size of the boat to which it will be attached. A huge board on a small vessel looks foolish. A tiny board on a large yacht is a kind of wasted effort. You don't have to guess at size, though, if you follow a simple formula: one inch of nameboard for each foot of the boats overall length. For example, a 40 foot trawler will look right with a 40 inch board on the port and starboard. If you are mounting the board on a sailboat, make it about 75% of the transom width. A powerboat will call for about 60% of the transom width. And it all depends upon the age and style of the boat, too. Since there are so many different boat designs, there are certainly no hard and fast rules. Just use your common sense, look at the boat, try the formula and allow yourself to adjust the dimensions to suit the setting. Before committing your design to wood, you could tape a pattern on the boat, stand back and see what you think. In terms of nameboard depth, this will vary with length and style. A small board may only require a 1/2" of thickness, a medium-large one may require 7/8" or even $1^1/_8$". The height of the board and letters is determined by using common sense and sensible proportions.

There are several nameboard styles I use all the time because they're classics. I have borrowed some designs, but I have also modified patterns, as well as created my own.

As we discussed in the Lettering chapter, you can give any of these traditional boards a contemporary look with your choice of lettering styles. Fantasy is particularly suited to a modern craft. You can also paint the boards instead of varnishing them.

Once you've decided the style and dimension of your board, check your board for straightness on both long sides. I feed a board through my tablesaw to establish a straight side; then, I flip it over and cut the other side. If you have any worries about uniform thickness, you can run the board through a thickness planer. If you don't have a tablesaw or thickness planer, just find a good lumberyard where they do a conscientious job of providing quality millwork.

Once your board is cut to the proper size, take your selected pattern for the board design and enlarge it to 100% of the size of the finished project. Cut out the pattern, tape it to the board, insert smudgeless carbon paper between the board and the pattern, and carefully trace it onto the board. Now, you're ready to shape your nameboard blank.

At this point, I'm going to walk you through creating nameboard blanks for those represented in the first part of this chapter. You'll discover many similarities, but the differences bear mentioning.

AMERICA

Notice the different look obtained by using two different fonts *(photos A-1 and A-2)*.

Above, America in the Pegasus typeface; in University Roman below.

Take a pencil compass and measure the radius of your beltsander's front wheel and then draw the radius emanating from each corner as illustrated *(photos A-3 and A-4)*.

Cut out the radius on your bandsaw or you can clamp it to a bench and use a sabre saw *(photo A-5)*.

Place the blank in your bench vise and smooth out the saw marks with your beltsander using 80 grit sanding belts *(photo A-6)*.

Run a hand held router with a 45 degree chamfer or 3/8" roundover bit all the way around the surface edge of the front face of the nameboard. This bit of detailing gives you a more finished look and also eliminates the 90 degree, sharp edges which are inclined to make your finish deteriorate more quickly *(photo A-7)*.

Route a 1/8" radius on the back of all nameboard blanks. Make sure you don't leave sharp edges anywhere.

A WORD OF CAUTION about routers; this tool has a mind of its own and it will try to get away from you continually. Hold it firmly and carefully. Also, it throws a lot of wood chips at high velocity, so wear your protective eye goggles and a paper filter mask.

FANTASY

25 degree Helvetica lettering above; below 20 degree Times Bold.

These nameboard blanks are so similar that I'm describing them together. There is no pattern with these designs because it would be a waste of time and energy to make one *(photos F-1 and F-2)*.

These blanks have parallel right and left edges that are angled to the long sides. The only difference is the degree of angle with one being cut at 20 degrees and the other at 25 degrees.

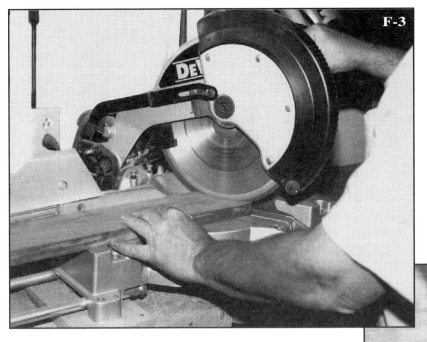

F-3

I draw a radius on the corners using the red cap off a can of WD-40. Cut this on your bandsaw or with a sabre saw and clean up all the edges and route a radius all around *(photo F-4)*.

F-4

You determine these angles with a simple protractor and draw the lines directly onto the boards. If you have a radial arm saw or a power mitre box, you can set it to the proper angle and be assured of identical cuts. If you only have a sabre saw or circular saw, just mark your angle using the protractor *(photo F-3)*.

I-1

INTREPID

The Intrepid style has been my most popular nameboard blank from the beginning *(photo I-1)*.

Measure and create a center line on the end of the board *(photo I-2)*.

I-2

I-3

HIGHER SKILL LEVEL NAMEBOARDS

The next group of nameboard blanks requires considerably more skill than the previous ones. As you could tell from the first group, there was nothing in the way of actual carving going on. The blanks we are now going to do will call upon the use of most of your handtools and more than a little technique. Beginners aren't advised to tackle any of these as a first project. However, if your dream is to just make one fine nameboard for your boat, the following instructions should help you achieve success in these carved boards if you are very patient and attentive.

Determine a radius that is pleasing to your eye and set your pencil compass. First transfer a line from the end of the board onto the center line. This point is the perfect spot to locate a countersunk hole for fastening the board to your vessel (photo I-3).

Set the point of your pencil compass on this crossed line and draw your radius (photo I-4).

Use a tri-square to draw the lines shown (photo I-5).

Cut towards the radius line first (photo I-6, page 13).

Starting at the end of the board, cut the radius towards your previous cut. Reverse the sequence to cut out the remainder of the radius (photo I-7, page 13).

Place the board in your bench vise and using files, rifflers, and sandpaper, clean up the saw marks on all edges. Route a chamfer or radius as you desire.

I-4

I-5

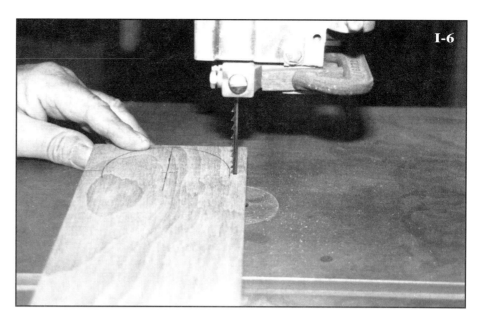

I-6

I-7

RELIANCE

The reliance nameboard is a simple ribbon board and relatively easy to carve *(photo R-1)*.

Convert the pattern to 100% of the size of the board you require and transfer the pattern to the wood. Cut out the shape with a band saw or sabre saw. Clean the edges using a beltsander, files, rifflers and sandpaper.

R-1

You'll notice the plane of the board end is 1/2 the thickness of the middle of the board. Use your two-handled router with a mortising bit to achieve this lower plane. Make sure you clamp the board firmly to your bench (photo R-2).

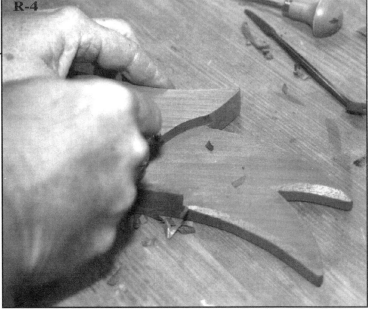

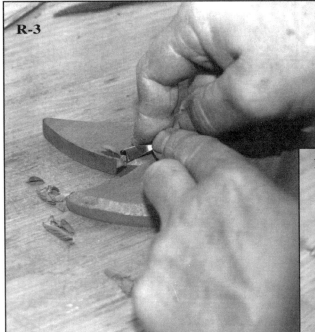

With your bent chisel, carve a chamfer on the sharp edges in preparation for rounding over these edges later (photos R-3, R-4 and R-5).

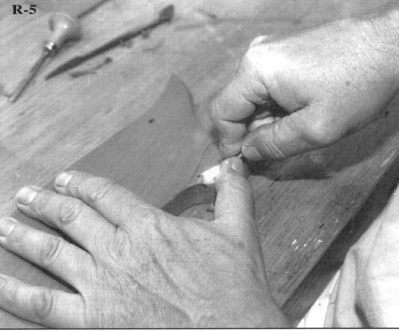

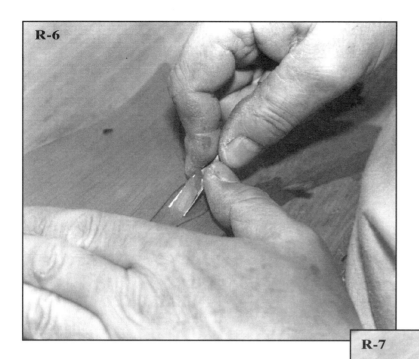

Begin to carve the scroll area down, using your #5 and/or your #7 swiss palm handled gouges. Watch closely for grain changes *(photos R-6 and R-7)*.

Carefully study the following photograph *(photo R-8)*. I'm converging, very carefully, on an important grain change. During the previous cut (not shown) I felt the grain change, before any splitting occurred I flipped the board and now I'm carving back towards the first cut, from the opposite direction.

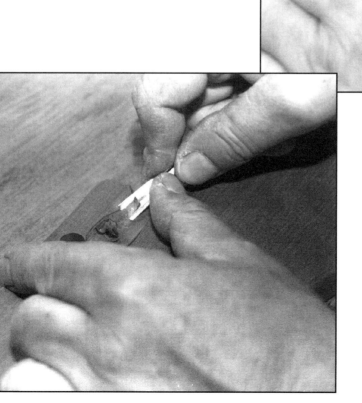

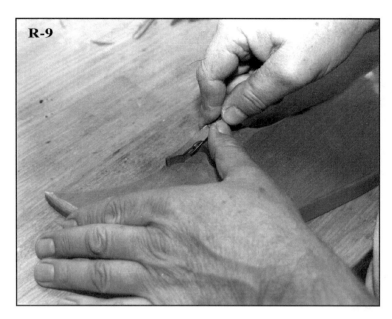

Now you want to start carving the ribbon down to the lower plane. Use your #5 or #7 gouge *(photo R-9)*.

With your #3 stubby gouge, carve a smoothly descending plane from the highest point to the lowest. You will find it necessary to carve off some of the pattern line between the two coves at this time *(photo R-10)*.

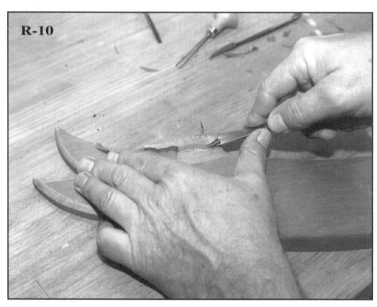

After achieving a smooth, descending plane, use your #3 gouge to cut the pattern line, at this point shown, at a 90 degree angle *(photo R-11)*.

Clean up the descending plane at the area where you just made the 90 degree cut. Use your #5 or #7 gouge and make sure you maintain the gradual descending plane *(photo R-12)*.

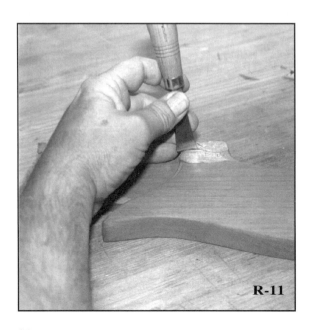

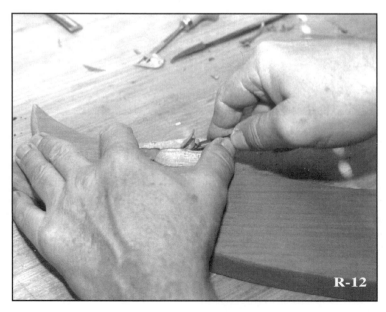

Using an assortment of tools, clean up the descending plane and the 90 degree vertical cut as shown. *(photos R-13 and R-14)*

With an assortment of rifflers, round over the edges where you had previously cut the chamfer *(photo R-15 and R-16)*.

Using folded squares of 80 grit sandpaper, clean up all tool marks and uneven cuts *(photo R-17)*.

R-13

R-14

R-15

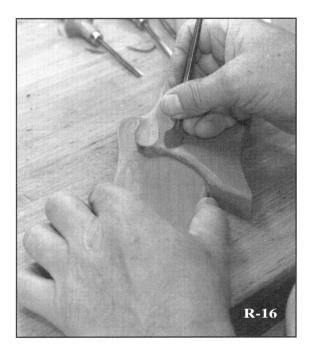

R-16

R-17

PURITAN / EASY GOING

This is one of the most traditional styles you can carve. Shapes similar to the Puritan and the Easy Going date back as far as nameboard carving itself (photos PE-G and PE-P).

Choose the fan or scallop you prefer from the pattern section of this book. Have it adjusted for the size you require using a copy machine that will enlarge or reduce.

Take the exact size pattern and tape it to the blank and trace it as we have done with other patterns. Cut the outside line of the pattern using a sabre, scroll or bandsaw. The pattern is transferred and the outside lines have been cut (photo PE-1).

Place the board in your bench vise and clean up the saw marks using a file, rifflers and sandpaper as needed (photo PE-2).

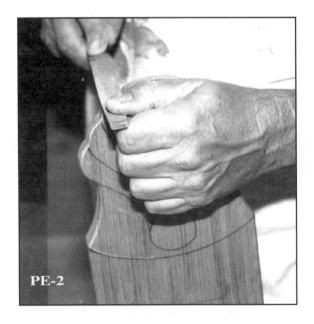

Place the blank on your bench and make a shallow angle cut as shown. Also, cut all your split-stops on all the lines as we have done in other projects (photo PE-3).

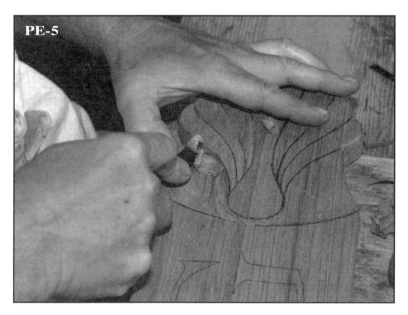

Using your 3/4" #3 Stubby Gouge start carving an angle down from the shallow cut that you carved in the preceding photo *(photo PE-4)*.

You keep carving this angle down, removing small amounts of wood with each pass. Keep recutting your split-stop at a 90 degree angle as you go to achieve about 1/2" of depth *(photo PE-5)*.

After you have carved this slope as smooth as possible, clean it up with a riffler *(photo PE-6)*.

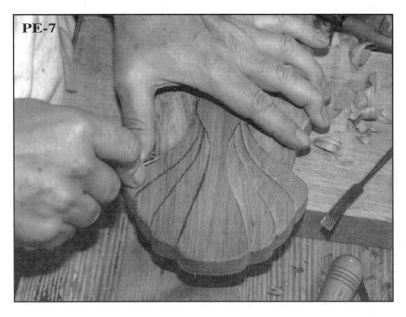

PE-7

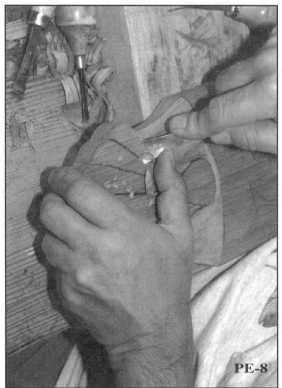

PE-8

Using your bent chisel, carve a radius on the first scallop or fan *(photo PE-7)*.

With your bent chisel and #3 gouge, carve into your split-stop at an even angle *(photos PE-8 and PE-9)*.

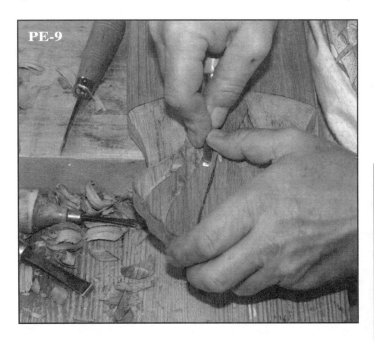

PE-9

Continue carving the scallops or fan as shown *(photo PE-10)*.

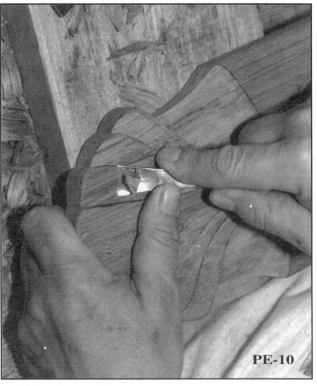

PE-10

Don't worry about carving across the grain; I do it all the time. Just make sure the edges of your gouge don't go beneath the surface of the wood *(photo PE-11)*.

Start with a shallow cut, using your #5 palm-handled gouge and carve out towards the end of the blank going only about 1/2". This is in reality a shallow cut split-stop *(photo PE-12)*.

Reverse the board and carve towards your previous cut *(photo PE-13)*.

Cross cut with your #3 gouge and work this area down to a shallow radius cut. *(photo PE-14)*.

Start cutting the end with your #5 palm gouge to desired depth *(photo PE-15)*.

Reverse the board and start carving back to the previous cut, use your #3 and #5 gouges as necessary *(photo PE-16)*.

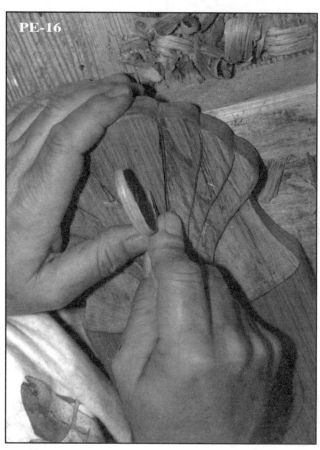

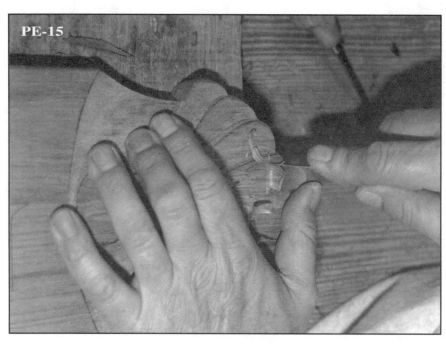

PE-17

After you have carved this area as smooth as possible, use a riffler to clean up all the tool marks *(photo PE-17)*.

PE-18

Clean all the tool marks out of all the cuts as shown *(photo PE-18)*.

Use 80 grit sandpaper to smooth even more *(photo PE-19)*.

PE-19

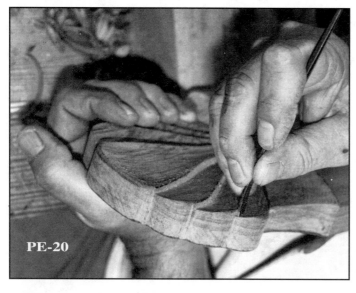

Clean up these edges with rifflers and sandpaper. Make a radius as you go along on all edges *(photos PE-20 and PE-21)*.

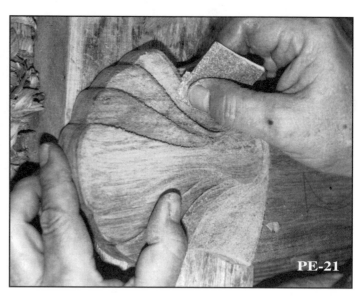

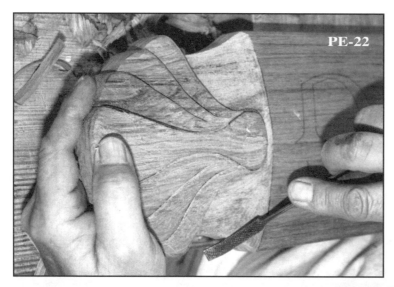

Now sand everything again with 80 grit sandpaper and go back over it with 100 grit sandpaper. You are now ready to carve the other end *(photo PE-23)*.

Continue to cut a radius on all the edges as you go along by using your riffler *(photo PE-22)*.

DEFENDER

The Defender is a classic style nameboard. The most difficult part of carving this style is that it has to be symmetrical. You must cast a wary eye as you carve (*photo D-1*).

D-1

Tape your pattern onto the blank and trace it on (*photo D-2*).

D-2

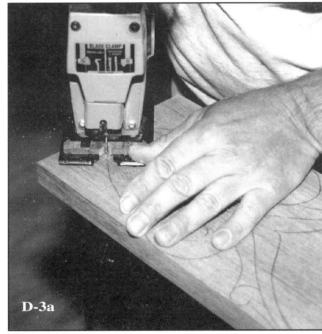
D-3a

Clamp the board securely to the workbench with C-clamps in a way that lets one end hang securely out in space. Put a block of wood between the clamp and the board because this will keep the nameboard from being dented. Take a sabre saw and cut only the outside line of the pattern as shown below. When you come to a place where you can't make a turn, back the saw out and come at it from a comfortable angle (*photos D-3a through D-3d*).

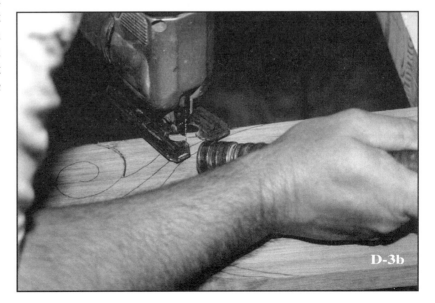
D-3b

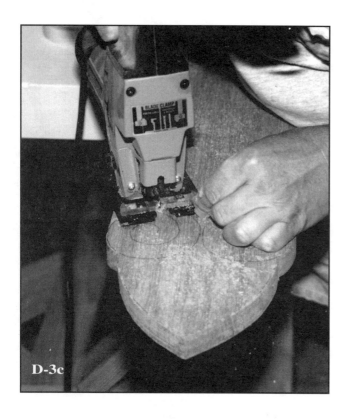

D-3c

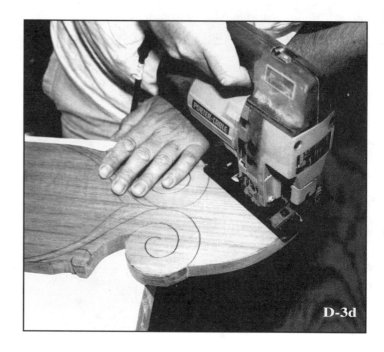

D-3d

D-4a

Clamp the board in your bench vise and sand all the edges with a beltsander fitted with an 80 grit belt. When you've smoothed all of the edges that you can reach with your sander, start to work smoothing other areas by hand. Power tools are great for speeding up the work, but they can't do as good a job as your hands in the areas where curves and angles meet. In fact, they can't do the job at all. Using an assortment of files, rasps, a folded square of sandpaper or any abrading tool, work to smooth the rough spots (*photos D-4a through D-4d*).

D-4b

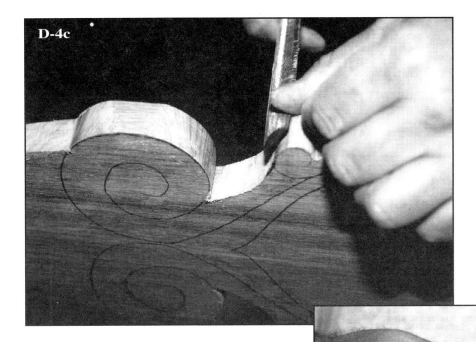

D-4c

D-4d

Power tools have one more major function in creating the Defender nameboard blank before you will be working entirely with hand tools. Clamp the board back flat on the bench with C-clamps, extending one end securely over the edge of the bench. Give yourself plenty of room for this "power carving" step. Study the design — a photograph is a great help — before you take the beltsander in hand. Notice that I have handcarved around the outside of the scroll and, using a gouge, I've brought that plane to the end of the board (*photo D-5*).

D-5

I can't tell you exactly how to do this because no one can. What I can tell you is that you're looking, taking in the level of rise and fall in the surface of the wood for the pointed element, and planning to duplicate it. Study the photographs repeatedly. You are seeking a sense of balance, a gradual flattening of the pointed element that will compliment the scrolls. If it is too thick, the board will look awkward and chunky. If it is too thin you risk it being snapped off either in your workshop or, much worse, on the boat.

Lay the beltsander on the pointed end of the board and sand to create dimension. You are rapidly removing material with this process and, believe me, you are saving a lot of time. Round the edges on the pointed plane, but not too much. You can always sand some more off, but you can't put wood back on. Study these photographs in succession (*photos D-5a and D-5b*)

D-5a

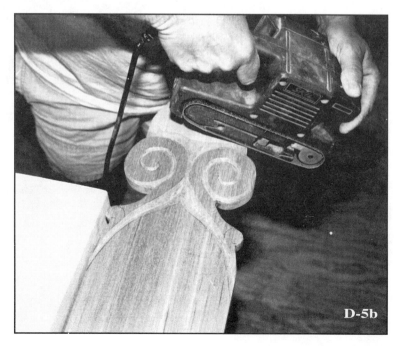

D-5b

D-5c

Begin to round the form as the plane arches up in the middle. Take it down to the scroll area. Continually compare it to the photograph and make adjustments as you sand a graceful descending plane (*photos D-5c and D-5c1*).

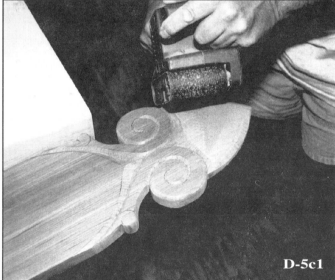

D-5c1

It's important to remember what you've done here because you're going to have to repeat it. If it varies somewhat from the photograph, don't be alarmed. As long as you have carved a pleasing shape, then your own creation will become the new pattern for the remaining end.

Keep sanding until you are satisfied with the graceful shape. Your hand is the best tool for feeling the proper shape (*photos D-5d and D-5d1*).

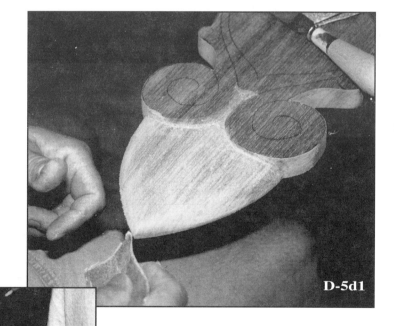

D-5d1

D-5d

THE SCROLLS

You've noticed that the beltsander hasn't gotten you very close to the scrolls. You can only approach these and finish the design with hand tools. Your pattern lines must be very distinct on the boards.

Select the handtools that will aide you in carving these scrolls. I often use several different gouges and my bent chisel to carve these scrolls and smooth it all out with rifflers and sandpaper squares. Study these photographs to understand the basics *(photos D-6 through D-10)*.

Once you've established the design in the wood, go back and fine tune it. Look for nicks and scraps and get rid of them. I make it a point to smooth out problem areas as soon as I see them. Be sure all of your rounded edges are actually round. Sandpaper away sharp edges.

D-6

D-7

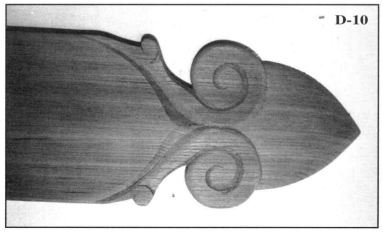

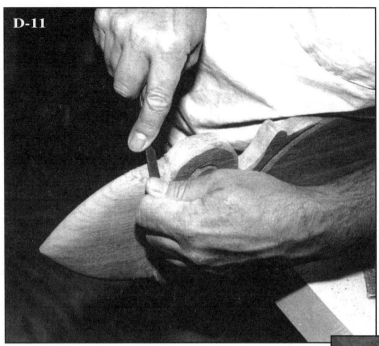

D-11

BRINGING IT ALL TOGETHER

Use this sequence of photographs to help you do your final shaping to the scrolls (*photo D-11 through D-16*)

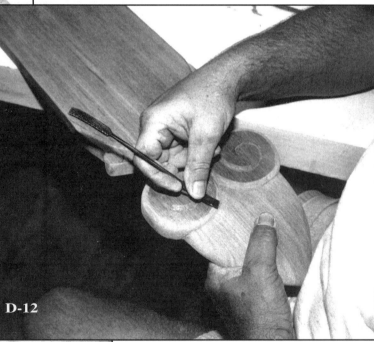

D-12

D-13

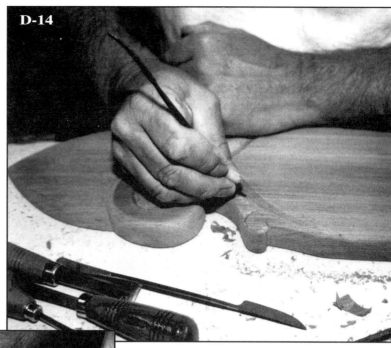

A FINAL CHECK

Cast a critical eye to the board and see if anything troubles you. Are your arches graceful, is your work as smooth as it could be, and does the design work well as a unit once all of the components are carved together? Keep your rasps, files and sandpaper handy *(photos D-17 and D-18)*.

D-17

D-18

Now that you've done a beautiful job, you get to do it all again on the other end. This project would probably take the average hobbyist quite a while to bring to this point. As I said in the beginning, it isn't easy. Once you've done it successfully, you're ready to carve any project.

D-19

COLUMBIA

This nameboard is one of my favorites. I created this by adapting different designs until I discovered an interesting combination *(photo C-1)*.

I've included a photograph of my first nameboard. I carved it for one of the boats I have owned. It's probably over 30 years old *(photo C-2)*.

As with the other boards, you've gotten a nice straight board, enlarged your pattern to fit and transferred it to the board with smudgeless carbon paper. Again, look at the photograph until you understand how

Put a 5/8" to 3/4" mortising bit into a two-handled sturdy router. The best router has a light built-in. Turn the router over and measure the distance from the router base edge to the outside of the bit. This will help you determine where to position the guide bar so that the router cuts well within the boundary of the lower line of the pattern. This line is about 3/8" from the top edge of the board and you want to" sneak" the router up to this line with several passes. You will need to move your guide strip and re-clamp it, but this is something you're going to have to do many times in the routing phase of this project *(photo C-4)*.

the different planes of depth are operating in this nameboard blank. Notice the fact that the letters are carved into a lower plane. Also, the Columbia has raised scroll work, similar to the Defender. Choose a board 7/8" to 1 1/8" because the carving will go as deep as 1/2" into the surface of the wood.

You're not going to cut out the outside of the pattern just yet; you will be using the board as a router table. Your first step will be to take a router to the center plane where the letters will be carved.

Lay the board on your workbench and secure it, along with a straight piece of wood the length of the nameboard blank and about 2" wide. Secure this using two large C-clamps at each end. This straight piece of wood will be your router guide *(photo C-3)*.

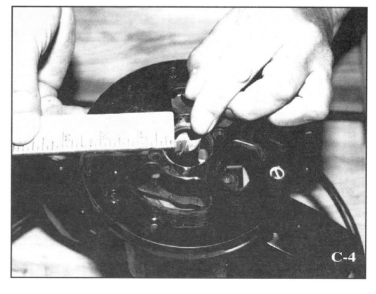

If your board is very long, you may need to install a block with screws against the center of the guide strip. **Safety note:** Put your goggles on for this router work. There is no other tool that throws as much wood-chips at high velocity as does a router (*photo C-5*).

With the router butted up firmly against the guide strip and holding it on a slight angle, start the machine and plunge the bit into the blank. Follow the guide strip until you reach the scroll area. When you reach the end of the pass, turn off the router and wait for the bit to stop rotating before taking it out. You are in tight quarters here and you don't want to take any chances with a runaway router. You can completely ruin an expensive piece of teak with even the slightest error. Re-set your guide strip, reposition your router and sneak ever closer to the pattern line. After several passes, you should be very close. Your final router cuts will be so minimal you can barely see wood chips flying, something very unusual for a router (*photo C-6, C-6a and 6b*).

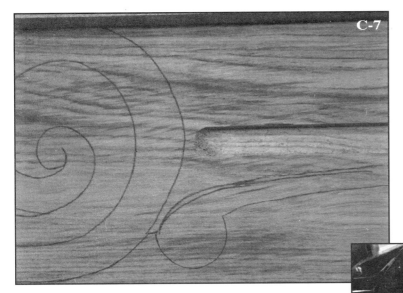

Take your time, pause when you get tired, and move the router in a zig-zag pattern up and down and left to right. This is like tacking a sailboat in a difficult wind. You'll move the router back and forth at about a

Unclamp and flip the board. Do the same process to cut inside the pattern line at the bottom of the design. Notice, though, that this line is only straight in the center section. You'll have to come back with hand tools to continue the arch to the left and right. In the meantime, make sure your C-clamps are very secure (*photo C-7*).

30 degree angle to the wood until the entire center plane becomes a uniformly deep plane. When you get to the left side, ease up close to the other scrollwork pattern line. Never try to cut more than half the diameter of the router bit when you are in this free-hand mode (*photo C-9 and C-10*).

Now, you have a pair of nice, uniformly deep, flat troughs running parallel to each other. Remove the guide strip and re-clamp the board. Taking your large, two-handled router, place it in the top right end of the top trough and start the machine. Eyeballing the scrollwork pattern line, bring the router close to it until you meet with the lower trough (*photo C-8*).

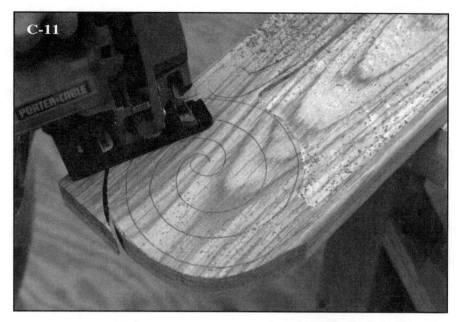

C-11

Clean up all edges with a beltsander. Hand file any ragged edges with a riffler or rasp. You want a small round-over on every edge so the board will hold varnish better after finishing *(photo C-12).*

Complete the scrolls and carving in the same way basically as you did with the Defender nameboard. These scrolls simply have a larger radius and will have broader surfaces, but the carving is essentially the same process. Naturally, carving is a very personal craft and you will pick your own method and tools instinctively after practice. Follow the sequence of photographs as you work *(photos C-13 through C-20).*

Next, un-clamp the board and slide one edge off the bench into the air. Re-clamp it securely. Using your sabre saw, begin the process of carefully cutting around the outside of the pattern. Move the board and re-clamp as often as necessary. Remember to use a blade that will easily follow the diameter that are cutting. Be prepared to back out and come from a new approach every once in a while *(photo C-11).*

C-12

C-13

C-14

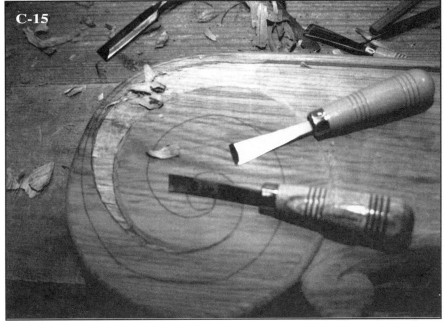

C-15

C-16

C-17

C-18

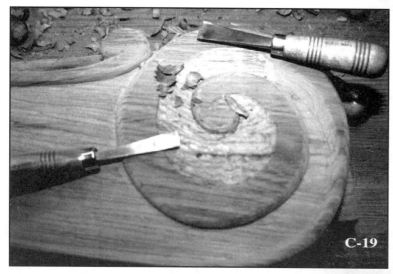

C-19

Sand the whole board, make any carving adjustments where needed. Pay attention to any scratches or tool marks and get rid of them (*photo C-20*).

C-20

SIDELIGHT & GRAND BANKS

The beauty of these nameboards is that they serve both a functional and decorative purpose. They hold the sidelights on a vessel. The illumination of running lights casts an appealing glow on the gold leaf in the lettering. These boards are a construction. Several separate wooden parts join with electrical hardware to create each one. Remember, you will make two of them, one for each side of the boat. They will be mirror images. Purchase your sidelights or lenses prior to starting this project. The parts you'll be making from wood should be built to accommodate whatever size sidelights or lenses you've bought. Refer to the measured drawings.

Built in Sidelight

Carve name prior to final assembly. Starboard side shown. Use mirror image for port side.

Fasten top and bottom through back piece and nameboard. Apply epoxy prior to screwing down. ***Dry fit first!*** *Route all face edged with 3/8" roundover bit after sanding. Route the 3/8" radius on edges of the pieces holding the lens prior to assembly.*

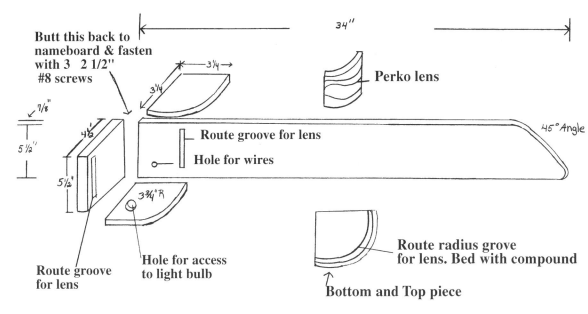

Butt this back to nameboard & fasten with 3 2 1/2" #8 screws

7/8"
5 1/2"
4 1/2"
5 1/2"
3 3/4" R

Route groove for lens

34"

Perko lens

Route groove for lens
Hole for wires

45° Angle

Hole for access to light bulb

Route radius grove for lens. Bed with compound

Bottom and Top piece

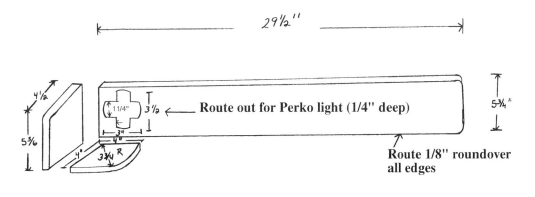

29 1/2"

4 1/2"
5 3/6
1 1/4"
3 1/2
3"
4"
4"
3 3/4 R

Route out for Perko light (1/4" deep)

5 3/4"

Route 1/8" roundover all edges

Grand Banks

Measurements are for board supplied by Grand Banks)

Use this basic design for any sideboard with a light shelf.

1/2" thickness is standard Grand Banks. 3/8" thickness optional

PRE-CURVED NAMEBOARDS

The transoms of many vessels have a radius or camber to them. If you try to install a flat nameboard by using blocks at the ends or saw scribes on the back of the board to compensate for the curve, you're going to have a less than satisfactory look.

Fortunately, there's a simple procedure you can follow to solve this problem. You simply pre-curve the wood by using two pieces glued together to match the camber.

Measure the curve or camber of the transom as shown in the illustration.

The assembled tools and materials that are used for this project are shown *(photo PC-1)*.

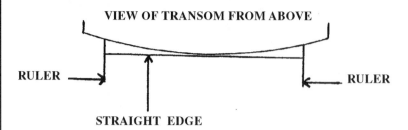

For pre-curving a board to fit the camber of your transom, you need the measurement as shown below:

VIEW OF TRANSOM FROM ABOVE

RULER →   ← RULER

STRAIGHT EDGE

Holding a ruler on each end of the straight edge, position it so that the center of the straight edge is on the center of the transom and both rulers show the same measurement.

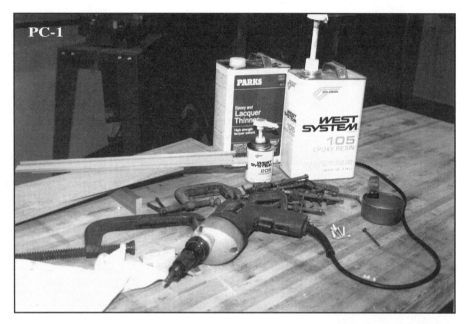

PC-1

In extreme curves, you will have to use three pieces of even thinner wood to be able to force the curve. In this case, the glued blank will not be flexible at all and you should use the exact measurements for best results.

1/2" thick teak and mahogany (normally called re-sawn 5/4 stock) is not readily available nowadays. You will probably have to purchase a 4/4 stock and mill it down.

If you have your own thickness planer be sure to use a dust mask and goggles for protection *(photo PC-2)*.

In this case, the nameboard blank we've chosen is the America. This requires using a 1/2" thick piece of wood for the face and a 1/2" piece for the back. There is going to be a lot of pressure required to glue these two boards together as a curve, so you're going to need a strong, solid bench to achieve good results. The finished size of the board we are doing in this project is 4"x24". Cut your 1/2" thick piece of wood for the bottom piece about 27" long. Cut a piece of scrap wood, in this case 1⅝", 1/4" more than the actual camber measurement, because the glued blanks tend to flatten when removed. In more severe curves, you'll have to add even more. A lot of times it is calculated guess work.

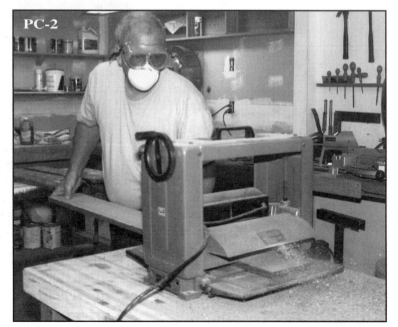

PC-2

Make sure to assist the wood out of the planer to avoid the cupping that usually occurs at the end of the board *(photo PC-3).*

Secure the bottom 1/2" piece of wood to the form. Pre-drill 3 or 4 holes at each end of the board about 3/4" from the edge *(photo PC-4).*

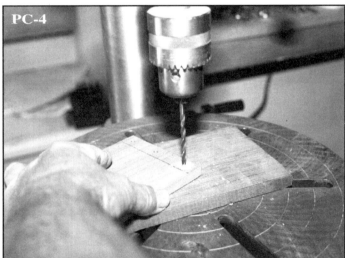

You'll need 1¼" #10 pan-head or round-head screws for the fastening. Screw one end to the bench as shown and position your block of wood slightly off center towards the end already secured to the bench *(photos PC-5 and PC-6).*

Now, you will need to force the other end down to the bench top. Us a C-clamp as shown and screw down this end. Remove the clamp *(photo PC-7)*.

Cut the 1/2" thick top piece about 25" long. Scratch the two faces of the boards that are going to be glued together with a sharp awl, nail or screw. Use a criss cross pattern of scratches *(photo PC-8)*.

Apply a liberal amount of epoxy to both scratched surfaces and even it out using a scrap of wood *(photos PC-9 through PC-9c)*.

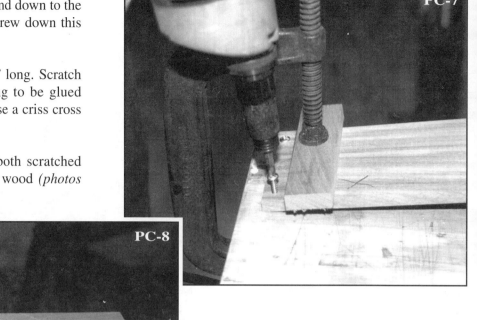

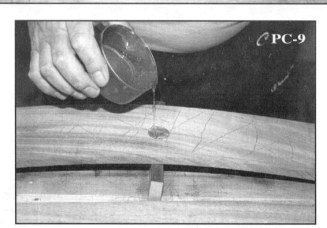

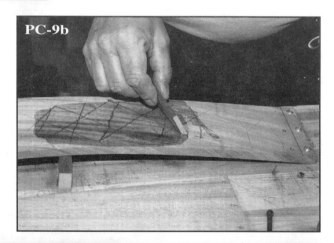

Place the two boards together, hold them parallel to each other, pre-drill and screw them together. Use a long enough screw so that it goes through both boards and into the bench *(photos PC-10)*.

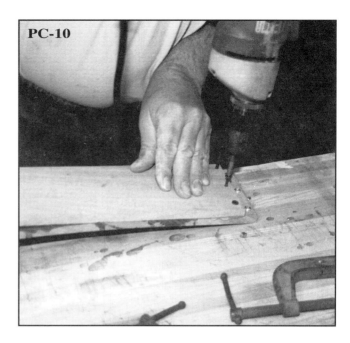

PC-10

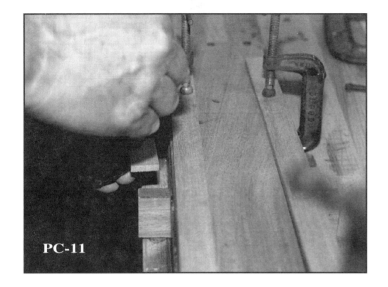

PC-11

PC-11a

Use C-clamps, one on either side, to hold the two boards together. Remember to use scrap pieces of wood between the clamps and the nameboard. Start clamping towards the center.

Keep adding C-clamps about every three or four inches along both sides of the boards until you have clamped down the entire board firmly as shown *(photos PC-11 through PC-11b)*.

PC-11b

When you have clamped as far as you are able to fit C-clamps between the bench and the two boards, take a large C-clamp, place a piece of scrap wood on the end and clamp it down tightly as shown *(photo PC-12)*.

Now drill and screw this end firmly down *(photo PC-13)*.

Clean up any excess epoxy with a rag moistened with lacquer thinner. Make sure there isn't any epoxy on the screw heads *(photo PC-14 and PC-15)*.

This is how the clamping should look.

Allow this to harden for 36 to 48 hours before removing the clamps and screws.

When you remove the glued blank from the bench, the edges won't be even and there will be hardened pieces of epoxy all over the edges and on the back of the blank. Also, the scraps of wood you used to protect the nameboard blank from the clamps and the piece of wood that you used to raise the blank to the proper curve will probably be glued to the back of the blank. Carefully snap off the ones that will come off easily using a chisel or hammer *(photo PC-16 and PC-17)*.

PC-16

PC-17

When you have finished preparing the blank and you are ready to carve the letters, you will notice that, because the blank is curved, it will not lay flat on your bench. It will be necessary to use a scrap of wood between the bench and the blank. This scrap is simply raising the nameboard blank off the bench enough so that you can have a flat surface under the board for carving. Move this piece of wood as necessary.

Be very careful not to apply too much force. If they don't come off easily, carve the scrap off, removing about half the thickness, and then remove the remainder using a belt sander *(photo PC-18)*.

I clean the board well enough at this point so that I can run the edges through the tablesaw to make the board edges parallel. At this point you can proceed with making the America blank as we did before, but this time, if you're using a bandsaw, mark your radius on the back of the board, or on the face of the board if you're using a sabresaw.

PC-18

LETTER CARVING

This is the part where the exercises you performed in Chapter V are going to start paying off. You've experienced virtually every grain change and carving method necessary to achieve successful letter carving. I'm going to show you a sequence of the carving steps for each of these 3" Times Bold letters. But first, we will look at transferring plots.

TRANSFERRING LETTERING PLOTS TO THE WOOD

Measure and mark the center of the nameboard and the center of the plot *(photo LP-1)*.

Do this same step to the other side. Double check that all your measurements are correct and secure the plot firmly to the board.

Insert your smudgeless carbon paper and transfer the plot to the board. Use a different color ink than you used on the plot because it will give an immediate clue about missed lines. A red pen is best for a blue lined plot. Press hard and outline every letter steadily as possible. If you're using the same plot for a pair of side boards use the red ink first, then black or blue ink for the second one *(photos LP-4 and LP-5)*.

Align the center marks and, using masking tape, temporarily tape the plot to the nameboard blank as balanced to the eye as possible *(photo LP-2)*.

Using a ruler, lift up the tape on one end and measure the top of the letter to the top of the board and the bottom of the letter to the bottom of the board. When both measurements are the same, re-attach the tape *(photo LP-3)*.

LP-4

LP-5

EMORS

These letters were chosen because they represent all the grain changes you'll experience in letter carving *(photo LC-1)*. Refer to the carving exercise to aid you if necessary. These photos are to be used as a guide during the carving progression. If you are unsure of yourself, re-carve the exercise in Chapter V.

LC-1

E - Use your butt chisels to cut your split stops *(photo LC-2)*.

LC-2

Now, carve these across grain cuts with your butt chisel *(photo LC-3)*.

Carve these with the grain cuts using your bent chisel *(photo LC-4)*.

The completed letter has been carved using only three tools, a 1¼" and a 1/2" butt chisels and your bent chisel *(photo LC-5)*.

M - Cut split stops *(photo LC-6)*.

The only difference between the M and the E is that you have "diagonal to the grain" cuts *(photo LC-7)*.

Continue carving down towards your bottom center lines *(photo LC-8 and LC-9)*.

With your bent chisel, carve the "with the grain cuts" *(photo LC-10)*.

THE COMPLETED LETTER

Remember to clean up the tool marks using rifflers and sandpaper *(photo LC-11)*.

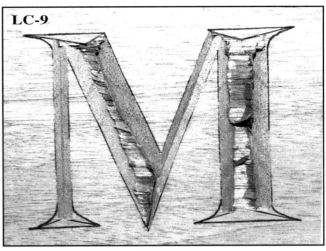

O - Cut split stops, refer to carving a circle in the exercise of Chapter V *(photo LC-12)*.

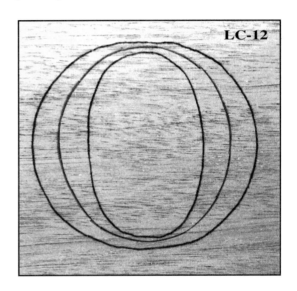

Use your bent chisel to carve these cuts on the inside of the radius *(photo LC-13)*.

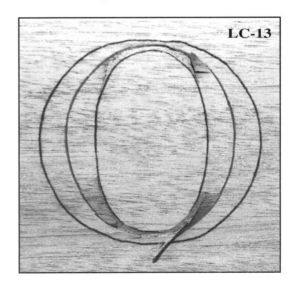

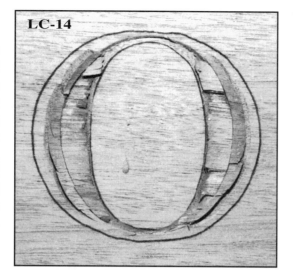
LC-14

Complete scribing a carved line on the inside radius with your bent chisel. With the bent chisel or the #3 gouge, remove some of the excess wood on the outside radius *(photo LC-14)*.

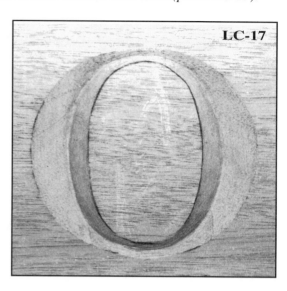
LC-17

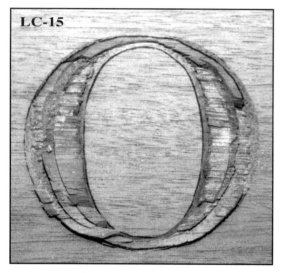
LC-15

R - Cut your split stops and notice that the letter "R" requires all the grain changes that you experienced in the carving exercise *(photo LC-18)*.

LC-18

Cut the scribe line on the entire outside radius line with your bent chisel *(photo LC-15)*.

Keep carving down using a combination of your bent chisel and #3 gouge *(photo LC-16)*.

Carve to this point using your butt chisels *(photo LC-19)*.

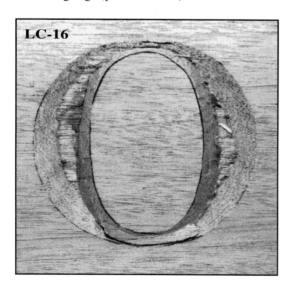
LC-16

LC-19

Carve to this point with your bent chisel *(photo LC-20)*.

THE COMPLETED LETTER *(photo LC-21)*.

S - Cut your split stops using your 1/2" butt chisel and your skew *(photo LC-22)*.

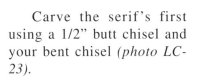

Carve the serif's first using a 1/2" butt chisel and your bent chisel *(photo LC-23)*.

Remove excess wood with your bent chisel *(photo LC-24)*.

Continue to carve deeper with your bent chisel. *(photo LC-25)*.

THE COMPLETED LETTER *(photo LC-26)*.

CARVING SCRIPT

My customers are constantly amazed that I don't charge extra for carving script. From my viewpoint, there is no reason to.

Script carving is no more difficult than block letters. In some ways it is actually easier.

Script is most often not carved as deep as block letters, therefore you have to exert less energy during the carving. All that is required is a little more finesse. When gold leafing time comes, the shallower letter uses less gold leaf than a block letter on the same size nameboard blank.

As always, cut your split stops. You'll notice in this photograph that I've made one continuous cut from the top of the letter "A" all the way down to my first grain change with my bent chisel *(photo S-1).*

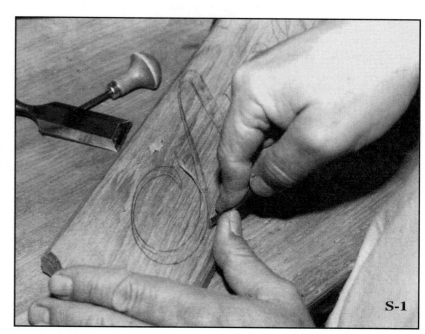

This photo illustrates an interesting carving technique. I'm using my #5 palm handled gouge in the same manner that I would use my bent chisel for carving the pattern line on a tight radius. The reason for doing this is that the descending plane at this point on a script letter is much less than 45 degrees, and this tool allows me to carve this descending angle much more easily *(photo S-4).*

Carving script is not that hard. Just continue carving your nameboard, adding the all important split stops as shown *(photo S-5).*

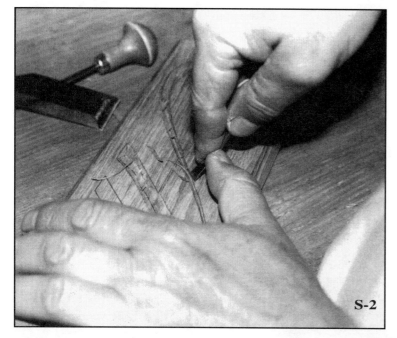

I now flip the board and make a single continuous cut in the opposite direction *(photo S-2).*

Even though I'm carving script, there are places that have straight cuts. I use my butt chisel the same as if I were carving a block letter *(photo S-3).*

S-4

S-5

SL-1

CARVING SMALL LETTERS

Small block or script letters require less force than large letters and a lot more finesse.

You'll notice that, on this 1" Times New Roman letter, I'm using one of my micro carving chisels to cut the serif split stop on the "R" *(photo SL-1)*.

SL-2

In this photograph, I'm using my #5 gouge to cut the radius split stop. I'll also go ahead and use the same tool to cut the descending angle from the outside pattern line, down to the center line at the bottom of the letter *(photo SL-2)*.

You'll notice that, on this small script "A", I'm using one of my micro gouges to carve a tight radius cut. I used my bent chisel to carve the other cuts seen here and I'll use my #5 gouge to cut the outside radius pattern line on the tail end of the "A" *(photo SL-3)*.

SL-3

CARVING LARGE LETTERS

7" TIMES BOLD R & S

When you start carving letters taller than 5" in height, some new problems will arise.

One of the first you'll encounter is doing "across the grain" letters, such as an "I". It's too difficult to handle a butt chisel larger than 1½" wide, so you must place your chisel on the lines carefully and try very hard to control the angle you're cutting. (Use less than a 45-degree angle or your letter depth will be much too great.)

Any mis-cuts on the longer line you are carving will be very hard to clean up later. They will stand out. The most likely mistake you'll make is illustrated below.

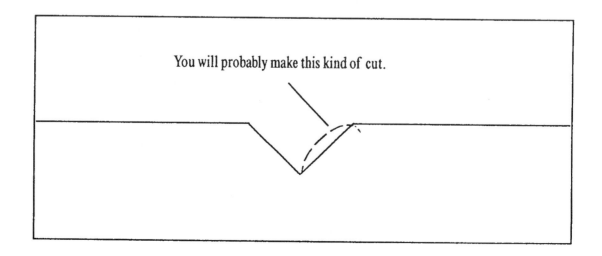

You will probably make this kind of cut.

Now don't worry about this too much. It's easy to smooth out this arch with a coarse riffler later. I would not try to recarve with your butt chisel. Just try to maintain a straight line down the center of the stroke. That's the most important aspect.

I chose the letters "R" and "S" because they represent most of the cuts you will encounter.

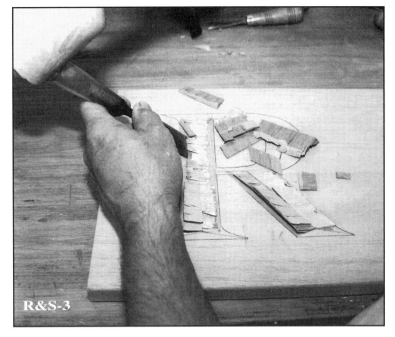

THE " R"

The first step is to cut your split stops as shown (*photo R&S-2*).

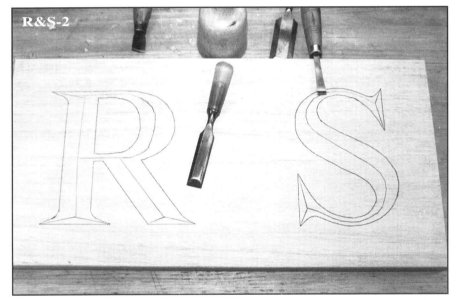

Use a 1¼" modified butt chisel to cut your 43 degree angle. Don't try to remove too much wood at a time — be patient. Keep turning the board to work down each side. Let the chips release themselves, don't pry them out *(photo R&S-3)*.

Use a 3/4" modified butt chisel to cut the inside of the radius *(photo R&S-4)*.

R&S-5

With a stubby 3/4" #3 gouge, remove the excess wood on the center of the letter. Stay away from the line of the outside radius *(photo R&S-5)*.

R&S-6

Take your palm-handled bent chisel and scribe the line of the outside radius. Cut a shallow angle and don't try to carve deep *(photos R&S-6 and R&S-7)*.

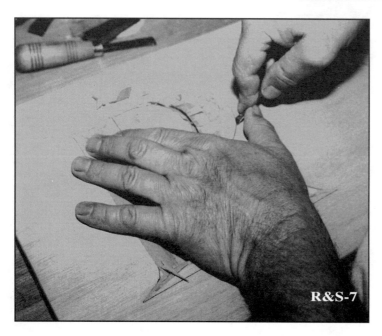

R&S-7

Keep re-cutting your split stop as you carve down. This will make it much easier to carve your angles. Use your 3/4" #3 gouge to help carve this plane down *(photo R&S-8)*.

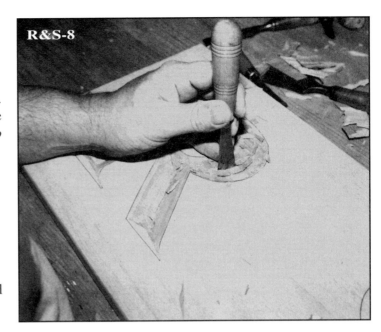

R&S-8

Clean up the tool marks left by the 3/4" butt chisel with your bent chisel *(photo R&S-9)*.

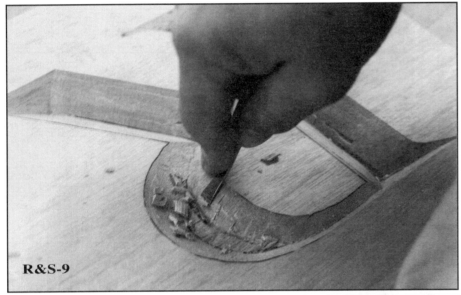

R&S-9

You might find it helpful to use your 3/4" butt chisel to smooth out the "with the grain cuts" *(photo R&S-10)*.

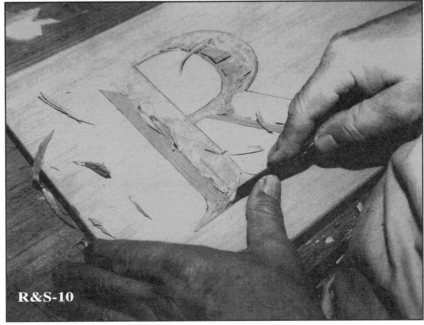

R&S-10

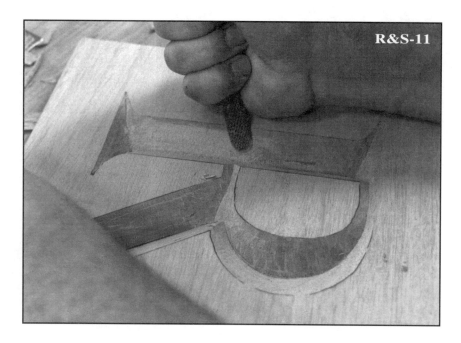

A sculptor's riffler is very helpful in cleaning up the tool marks *(photo R&S-11)*.

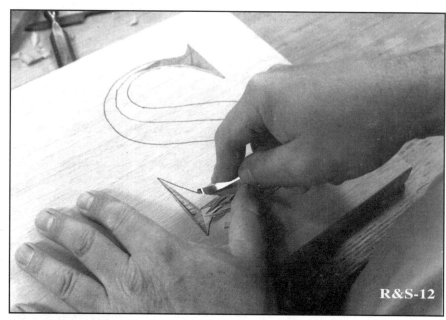

THE "S"

Cut your split stops and then start the letter by carving out the serifs first using your 3/4" butt and bent chisels *(photos R&S-12 and R&S-13)*.

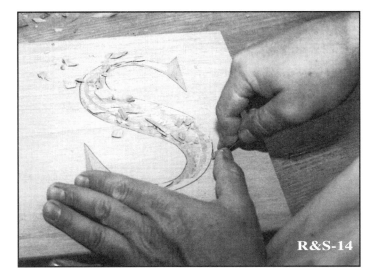

Scribe the lines of the "S" using your bent chisel *(photo R&S-14)*.

It's helpful to use your 3/4" #3 gouge to remove excess wood and then use it to re-cut your split stops. Since the "S" is a continuous radius this tool can be used to carve the plane down to the bottom of the letter *(photos R&S-15, R&S-16 and R&S-17)*.

The bent chisel is used to carve down at the straighter areas *(photo R&S-18)*.

The finished letter now needs to be smoothed out using rifflers and sandpaper *(photo R&S-19)*.

Fill the grain pull-outs with surfacing putty and, after that's dry, clean up the carving with 80 grit sandpaper *(photos R&S-20 and R&S-21)*.

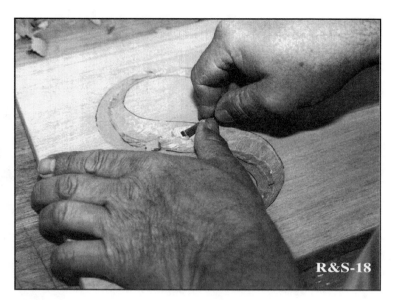

R&S-18

R&S-19

R&S-20

R&S-21

FASTENING NAMEBOARDS
TO A VESSEL

There are three methods of accomplishing this task:

1. The most common is to drill counter sunk holes on either end of the nameboard prior to finishing. You drill them at this time so that the epoxy and varnish that are applied penetrate the hole.

If you drill these holes after finishing, the finish will deteriorate very quickly around the hole and eventually will cause a major breakdown of the finish.

I use Phillips, oval head, self-tapping, stainless steel screws or bolts. If the nameboard is varnished, I spray paint the screw or bolt heads brown prior to installation.

If you carve a star in your nameboard that's been gold-leafed, take one of those pre-painted screws and gold-leaf it. (Refer to the gold-leafing chapter.)

Please don't use finishing washers; their sharp edges will break the varnish seal on the face of the board.

2. Another method of fastening the nameboard is to pre-install a bolt hole prior to finishing. The method I use is to drill with a Fuller brand counter bore on each end of the nameboard through the face.

I then flip the board over and drill a shallow counter bore on the back. At this point, I pre-install the bolt through the face. Usually using ¼" 20 nuts and bolts. I now put a dab of epoxy in the counter bores on both sides and take a screwdriver and pull the nut into the counter bore on the back as firmly as possible.

I then install a teak or mahogany plug or bung into the surface counter bore and sand it flush.

Make sure you have enough bolt length out of the back of the board so that you can install it in your desired location using lock washers and nuts.

3. The third method is to screw out from the boat into the back of the board. This is potentially the the most difficult way to install because you have to be very careful in selecting the length of the screws you use.

If the screws are too short, the board may fall off. Conversely, if they are too long, they will break through the face of the board.

If you select this method use a #12 or even a #14 self tapping screw. Drill through the boat using a bit that is slightly larger than the screw and drill into the board with a bit that is about the diameter of the shaft of the screw excluding the threads.

Be careful not to locate the screws where there are carved letters.

Regardless of which method you choose, install a fender washer or rubber washer between the board and the boat. Since the back of the board has at least two coats of epoxy on it, water won't penetrate the wood.

This method of keeping the board slightly away from the boat has advantages. If you install the board tight against the boat, the back of the board will have to be completely covered with bedding compound. This is not only messy, it will cause substantial discoloration to the boat's finish.

In keeping the board away from the boat you will avoid this messy operation by allowing water to drain away and air to circulate.

My advice for any nameboard installation is that it become a two-person task. One can stand back and make sure everything is aligned visually and, as the other holds the board, the first person can come forward and mark the location of the board on the boat.

CHAPTER 7
EAGLES

Eagles have a long history in woodcarving. No doubt this is because the eagle is a nearly universal symbol of power and freedom. Ancient cultures, such as the Egyptians, Native Americans, and European explorers all used their versions of the eagle in ceremonial contexts to symbolize strength. Many a ship, especially those with a military mission, has been adorned with a fierce eagle.

I really enjoy carving eagles because there are so many possibilities. You can carve *bas relief* eagles that stand — or fly — alone or you can incorporate them into elaborate designs involving shields, arrows and ribbons. Eagle heads can be used to decorate tillers.

I'm not an artist, so I don't draw my own eagles. Instead, I go in search of patterns that were created a long time ago. I may borrow one element from one pattern and one from another until I create an overall design that fits the space and purpose of an eagle project.

There are patterns of several eagle designs in the Patterns and Designs chapter of this book, to give you an idea of the possibilities. You can also check with your reference librarian to find more sources and examples.

I'm going to carve my rendition of the Bellamy Eagle first, the least complicated eagle I carve. Then, I'll do a more elaborate eagle with a shield and ribbons that is a construction. The third eagle is what I call Jake's Eagle (Jake is my young son to whom this book is partially dedicated.) This eagle is, in fact, a 19th century polychrome eagle I located in *The American Eagle in Art and Design* by Clarence A. Hornung (Dover Books). This book is an excellent resource for eagle design.

Everything you need to know about eagle carving is included in this chapter. These are ambitious designs, so you need to feel confident about your woodworking and handcarving skills for these projects.

THE BELLAMY EAGLE

John Bellamy was a late 19th century ship decorator from Maine. I came across an eagle of his and decided I wanted to modify it. I give credit to Mr. Bellamy for the original inspiration *(photo BE-1)*.

BE-1

To tell the truth, I first carved this eagle in 1969 and I have forgotten a lot about why my version looks the way it does. I would love to know who designed this version so I could give them credit.

I'm going to give explicit instructions about the steps necessary to complete the Bellamy Eagle. For the rest of the eagles in this chapter, you'll need to come back and refer to this chapter for several steps.

This is a construction in two parts. The head and beak are on an oval-shaped piece that will be epoxied on during the project.

I am working with a 1 1/8" piece of mahogany for my particular project. When the carved head is attached, there will be considerable depth near the top of the eagle. The effect is very dramatic.

Refer to the Patterns section of this book for a pattern you can take to your copier shop and enlarge to a size that appeals to you.

The one I am working on in the photographs has a 34" wingspan.

Transfer the major lines of your pattern to the wood using smudgeless carbon paper. You're going to have to cut the pattern later on, so be sure to save it *(photo BE-2)*.

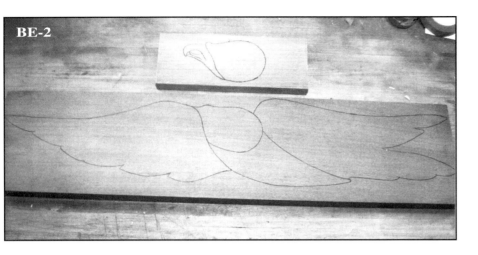

BE-2

Cut out the outline of the body portion with a bandsaw or sabre saw *(photo BE-3)*.

Take your beltsander and sand all of the edges clean. Place the mahogany section into your bench vise for easy handling during this step. After you have cleaned up the edges, use a 1/8" roundover router bit to put a radius on the front and back to help avoid splitting that may occur with sharp edges. Don't route the top edge of the body where the head will be glued on at a later date *(photo BE-4)*.

BE-3

BE-4

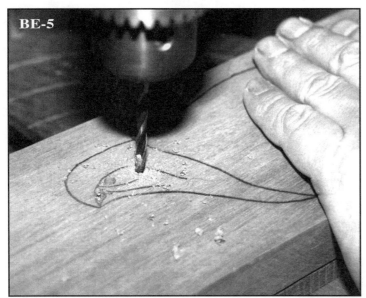

I always like to work on my eagles head first. The head, especially the eye and the beak, determine the character of a carved eagle.

Prior to cutting out the pattern, use your drill press to drill small diameter holes at the corners of the mouth *(photo BE-5)*.

Then use larger diameter drills to remove most of the wood in this area. Be careful not to drill outside the pattern lines *(photos BE-6 and BE-7)*.

BE-8

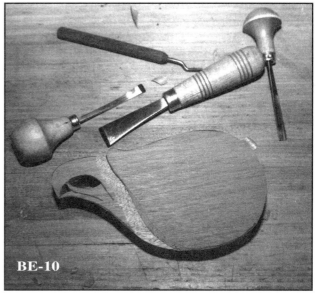

BE-10

Cut out the head and neck with a bandsaw or sabre saw *(photo BE-8)*.

Then, hold and rotate the edges of the eagle's head on the beltsander so that you create a nice smooth plane. Don't route a radius on this piece *(photo BE-9)*.

Carve out the line between the neck and the beak, as shown *(photo BE-10)*.

Firmly attach the head to a carver's work positioner, or clamp it to your bench in a way that the neck area overhangs. Use a beltsander to shape the neck in a descending arch as shown *(photo BE-11)*.

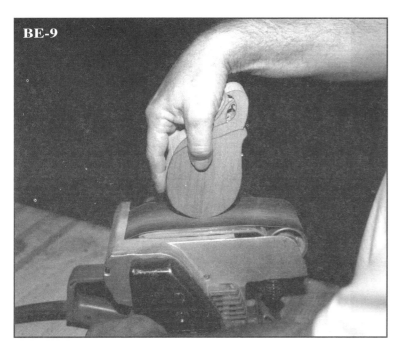

BE-9

BE-11

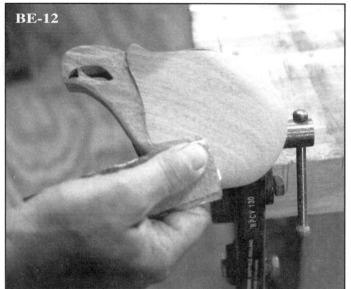

BE-12

Now, put the head piece aside and let's get to work on the shield and wings. We will get back to the detail on the head after it is glued onto the body of the eagle. This will act as a work positioner when carving the detail.

Screw the wings and shield to your work positioner with the back of the eagle facing out. Be sure to place the screws onto the area where the head will be glued. Use a beltsander to arch the plane of the wings away from the center of the body. This process adds a little dimension to the overall shape (*photos BE-15 and BE-16*).

Use 36 and/or 50 grit sandpaper squares to smooth out the neck and beak (*photos BE-12 and BE-13*).

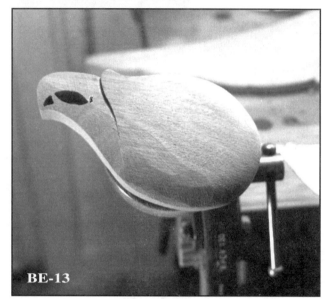

BE-13

Take your beltsander and using the technique shown, sand the back of the beak down at an angle towards the point of the beak (*photo BE-14*).

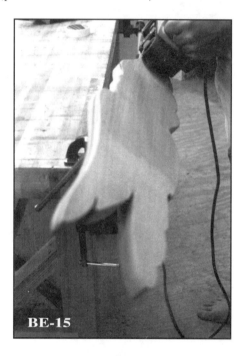

BE-15

BE-14

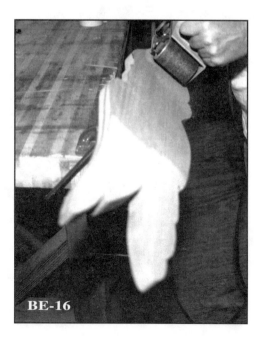

BE-16

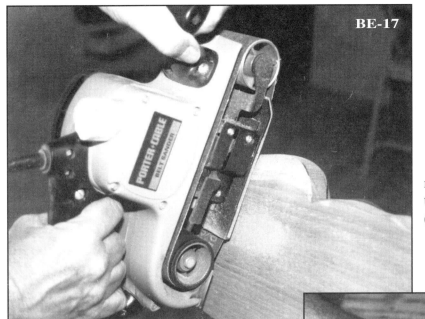

BE-17

Again, with a beltsander, power carve the rough radius to the top edge of the wings and then clean the radius with a hand file and riffler *(photos BE-17. BE-17a and BE-17b).*

BE-17a

BE-17b

Remove the wings and shield from the work positioner and rough carve a dividing line between the shield and head gluing area. This will assist you in avoiding mistakes in the upcoming power carving step (photo BE-18).

Re-attach the wings and shield to the work positioner and draw a guide line to assist you in power carving a flowing slope to the shape of the wing plane. This line is just a guide, shape the edge and plane of the wings with a beltsander to a form that is pleasing to your eye. Use a larger belt-sander with 50 grit belts to sand cross-grain and a smaller one to shape with the grain (photos BE-19 through BE-22).

BE-18

BE-19

BE-20

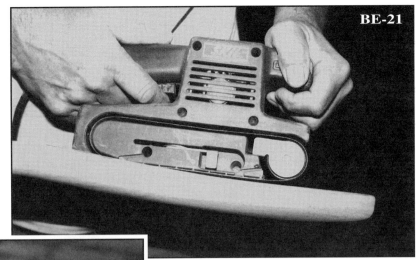

BE-21

You are now ready to shape the wings with your power grinder. Don't use a disc any coarser than 50 grit. (If you don't have any experience using a angle grinder, practice on a scrap board first. This tool removes a lot of wood fast.) In a flowing motion, never stopping the movement of the tool, grind the cove area of the wings as shown (*photos BE-23 and BE-24*).

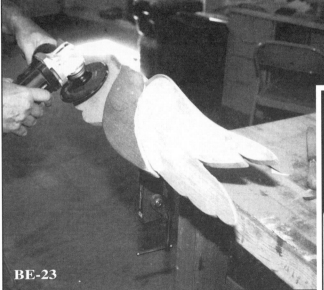

BE-23

BE-24

Remove the eagle from the work positioner and return to your carving bench. Begin the hand carving stage of roughing out the cove at the top of the wings. In the photographs, I'm using a stubby bent gouge, and long-handled Swiss fishtail #5 gouge (5F/20). Be very careful to watch and listen for grain changes. You can usually assume that if you are carving either cross-grain or with the grain "down hill" that you are safe against splitting, but still be careful. I use quite a few cross-grain cuts while carving the wings (*photos BE-25 through BE-28*).

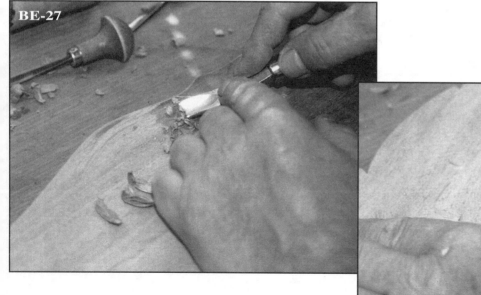

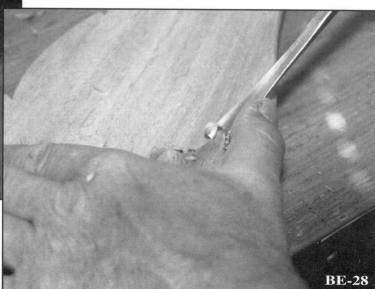

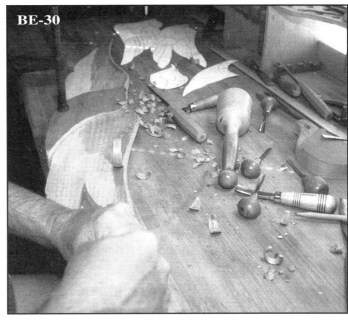

Being very careful to feel the direction of the grain, use your #3 stubby gouge and the long-handled #5 fishtail gouge to carve the cove along the top edge of the remainder of the wings *(photos BE-29 through BE-31)*.

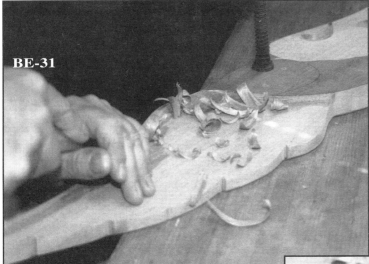

With the eagle firmly clamped to your bench, holding your #5 fishtail gouge in a reversed position so that it will carve a radius rather than a cove, rough shape the outside edge of the shield *(photo BE-32)*.

Use a beltsander to shape the flatness out of the shield and to put the final radius on the edge *(photo BE-33)*.

Now you'll want to clean up any tool marks and work the plane of the wings using a coarse sculpter's riffler and 36 and 50 grit sandpaper. I've assigned the riffler to my 3½-year-old son, Jake, and I'm using the sandpaper *(photo BE-34)*.

Assuming that you're going to proceed with the head, now is the time to finish carving the back or inside of the beak. Using an assortment of tools, rifflers and sandpaper, define the shape of the beak as shown *(photo BE-35)*.

BE-33

BE-34

BE-35

After you have completed the back of the beak, glue or epoxy the head onto the body. Be extremely careful in your alignment of the head. Allow the project to be clamped together overnight.

The next morning, trace the head and neck pattern onto the wood (*photo BE-36*).

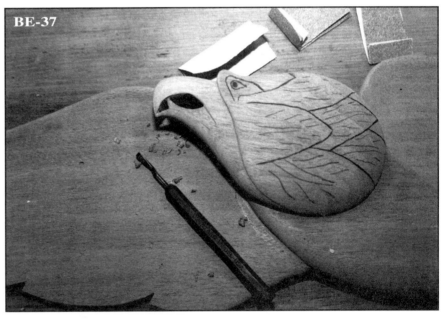

With an assortment of your micro dogleg chisels, sandpaper and smooth cut rifflers, shape the beak and tongue to final form (*photo BE-37*).

Using an assortment of your micro gouges, carve out the eye. If you choose to do this project with a 34" wingspan as I did, be extremely careful here. The more open grain of the mahogany leaves you in a position where the raised semi-circle of the eyeball can easily break off (*photo BE-38*).

BE-39

With a variety of tools, carve out the plane and detail around the eye *(photo BE-39)*.

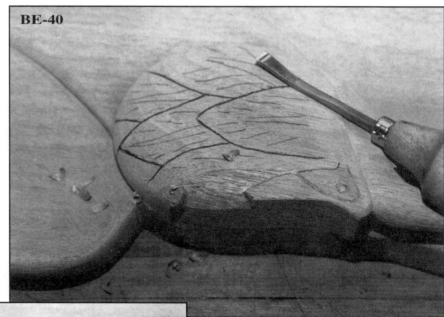

BE-40

Now carve the arched plane of the top of the head and the feather detail *(photos BE-40 and 41)*.

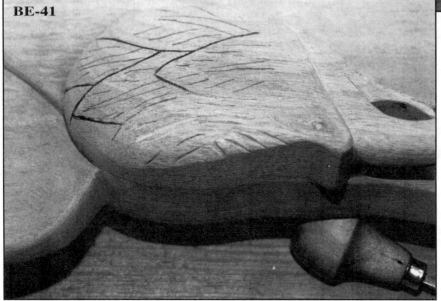

BE-41

BE-42

At this point, complete carving the feather detail on the head. With rifflers and sandpaper squares, clean up the tool marks and smooth out the planes and radii as needed *(photo BE-42 and BE-43)*.

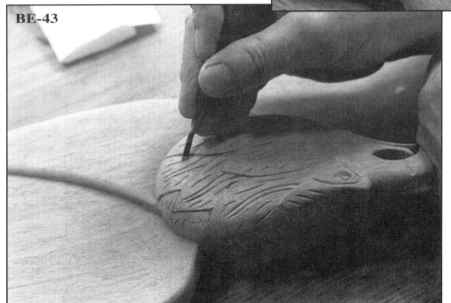

BE-43

Using the patterns that you have cut to fit, transfer the major lines of the shield and feathers onto the wood *(photo BE-44)*.

BE-44

I've chosen to carve the detail into the shield at this point. Using one of your micro gouges, carve a cove into the banner, following the pattern lines. You can make a continuous cut without much thought about grain changes with these very sharp tools, but you must be very attentive to not allow the points of the gouge to penetrate the surface plane. Use a micro dogleg chisel to carve the stars (*photo BE-45, BE-46 and BE-47*).

After you have completed the shield, you can begin carving the "stepped" effect to the feathers. You will need an assortment of tools to accomplish this.

I always start at the highest point and work "down hill," so that I can be somewhat confident that I am carving with the grain *(photo BE-48)*.

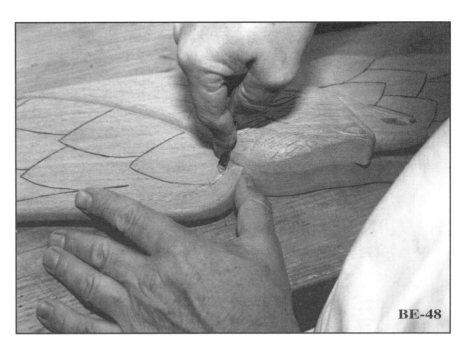

BE-48

You will find it necessary to clean out these tight corners, using your micro dog-leg chisels, in an "against the grain" cut. Proceed very carefully, carving multiple shallow cuts, rather than one deep cut *(photo BE-49)*.

BE-49

BE-50

Study the following sequence of photographs so that you are able to visualize how the progression of the "stepped" effect continues *(photos BE-50, BE-51 and BE-52)*.

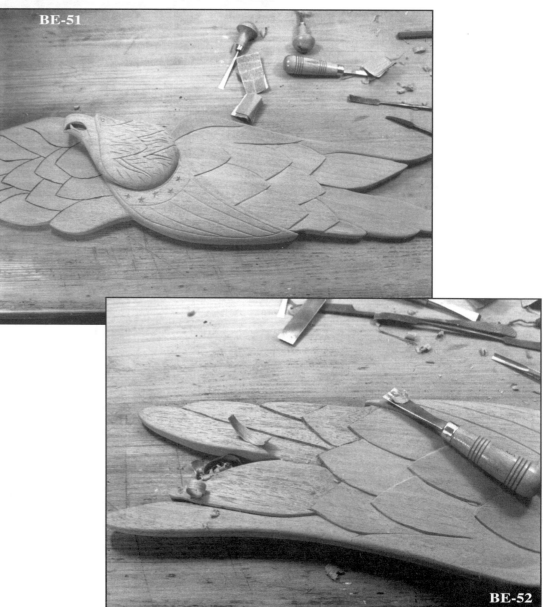

BE-51

BE-52

After you have done quite a lot of riffler and sandpaper smoothing on the first half, start carving the "stepped" effect on the other wing *(photos BE-53 and BE-54).*

BE-54

BE-53

You have now completed the "stepped" effect on both wings while making sure that you have carved and smoothed out the planes and edges on all the feathers.

With a sharp pencil, hand draw in the feather detail, while referring to your pattern.

Now you are ready to carve the spines and V-grooved feather detail.

I use my palm handled bent chisel to cut my split stops as well as the V-grooves into the feathered spine.

Using small rifflers, clean up these cuts and sand a radius to the spine with sandpaper squares *(photo BE-55).*

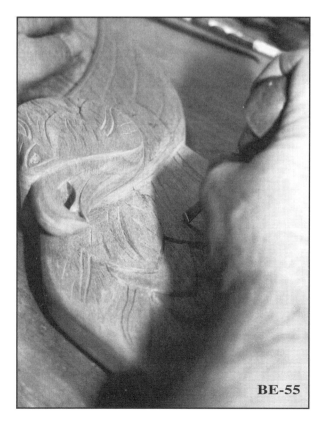

BE-55

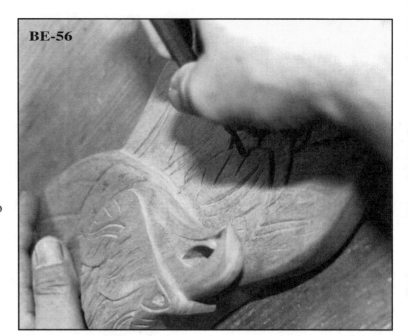

Use the appropriate size micro dogleg chisel to carve the V-grooved feather detail *(photo BE-56)*.

Carving in the feather detail is tedious work. Take your time and do the best job that you can. You have consumed a lot of time and effort to reach this stage.

View the following sequence of photographs to aid you in defining the look of the feather detail *(photos BE-57, BE-58 and BE-59)*.

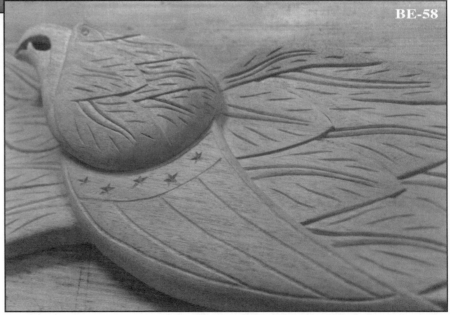

Now sit back and admire the great job you have done. I leave the eagle unfinished for several days so that I can fine tune the details and because I enjoy the feel of the natural wood *(photo BE-60)*.

EAGLE AND SHIELD
WITH TWO RIBBONS

ES-1

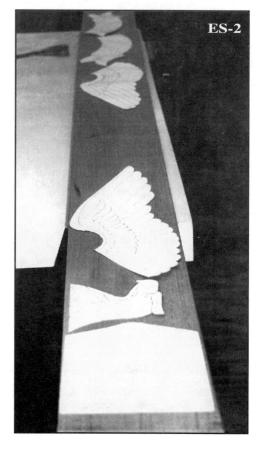

ES-2

This is a very large construction meant for display on a boat of considerable size or, as I have used it, as a sign advertising my business at trade shows.

While the previous project, the Bellamy Eagle, is a construction, this is much *more* of a construction. The Bellamy has two parts; this one has seven. I'm not going to go over this project in the same detail as the Bellamy Eagle because you can refer to that section for information on carving.

I selected a 14-foot board of mahogany. On a project of this size, mahogany has two features going for it over teak: it's a cheaper and a softer wood, which makes it easier to carve. This board is 7¼" wide by 7/8" thick. My task is to create a design that will fit comfortably on this board. As you can see from the photograph, I decided to do an eagle head, uplifted wings, a shield with stripes and stars, a ribbon at the top and a ribbon on the bottom. All of the components were designed prior to 1930. These components will be carved separately and pre-assembled prior to finishing (photo ES-1).

It's time to look at the board and place the pattern pieces on it to see where they fit. Before that, I run the board through the tablesaw along each edge to be sure both sides are parallel. It isn't necessary to square the ends because I'm anticipating some waste. Then, I place the pieces on the board, avoiding any area that seems suspect. Notice the open section with no patterns in the photograph. There is a grain swirl and knot there (photo ES-2).

Cut out all of the patterns apart using a radial arm saw. You can also use a circular saw.

Using a radial arm or circular saw, cut the straight line down the edge of the wings as shown. Using a band saw or sabre saw, cut out the entire wing pattern (photos ES-3 and ES-4).

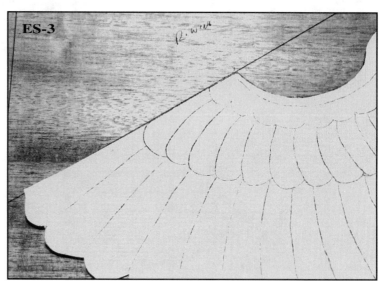

ES-3

ES-4

The eagle head and shield run at opposite grain directions on the board for a reason. The shield goes with the grain and the eagle goes against the grain — placing the beak with the grain — because you will have the best carving control with this configuration. Cut out these parts with a band saw or sabre saw. Cut out all of the other pieces in the same way *(photo ES-5)*.

ES-5

neatly and securely. (You can also use a dowling jig — a considerably less expensive tool. See the Tools chapter.) I line up the components to determine where they will be joined and make pencil marks on the surfaces where the joining will happen. Using the plate joiner, I create slots in each edge where two boards will come together. Do every pocket before going to the next component. Study where the wings fit on the shield. Insert the biscuits and see that the construction will fit together when the time comes to epoxy them. These photographs will help clarify what I mean *(photos ES-6 through ES-7c)*.

At this point, before the carving begins, it's time to prepare the construction for assembly. Porter Cable makes the ideal tool for the job. The biscuit joiner is absolutely the best and easiest way to prepare a construction that will hold together

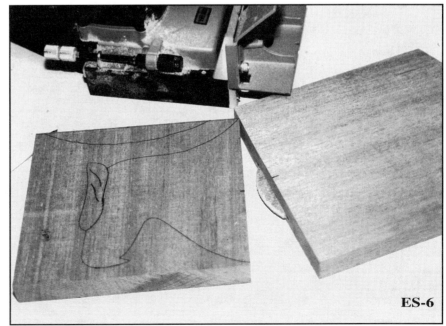

ES-6

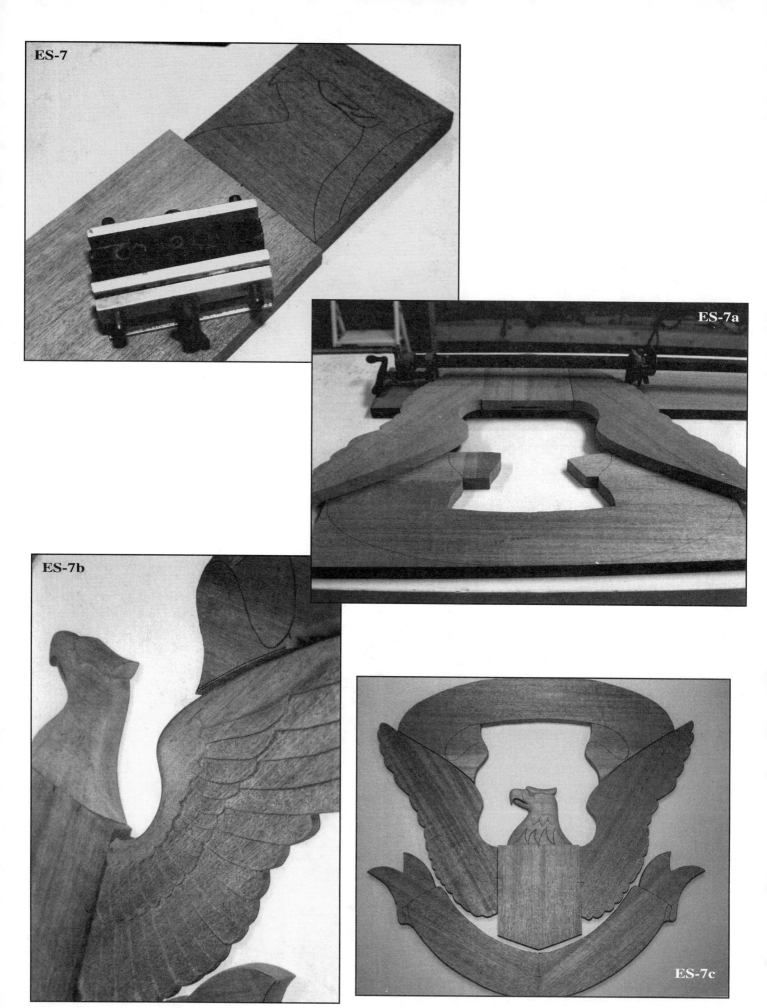

ES-7

ES-7a

ES-7b

ES-7c

Have you noticed the top ribbon is wider than the board? I simply take a piece of scrap with the same grain pattern and edge glue it together. I clamp it and let it set up for 24 hours. Then, I cut out the whole perimeter *(photos ES-8 and ES-9)*.

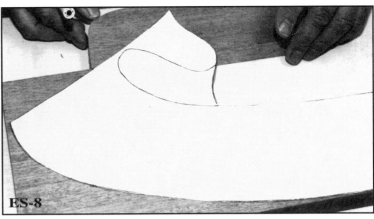
ES-8

ES-9

ES-10

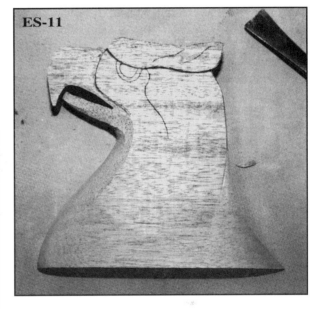
ES-11

The bottom ribbon won't fit either. I simply place the pattern on two pieces of wood, careful to create a nicely fitting angle between them. I glue them together with my biscuit joiner, Then, I cut out the perimeter of the whole pattern after the epoxy has set *(photo ES-10)*.

BEGINNING THE CARVING

I always start with a eagle's head, because that determines the "attitude" of the eagle. Carving an eagle is a personal thing, some may want a fierce look while others may desire a friendlier tone to the carving.

Consider how the eagle is going to look when it sits atop the shield. It's not going to sit like a static block. The eagle's breast is rounded, but will still need to maintain almost the same depth as that of the shield *(photo ES-11)*.

Clamp the eagle's head upside down in a bench vise. Using a beltsander, shape the neck as much as possible *(photo ES-12)*.

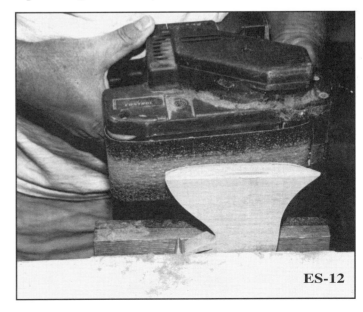
ES-12

Turn the eagle's head in the vise and using assorted files, rifflers & sandpaper create nice smooth edges all around (photo ES-13 and ES-14).

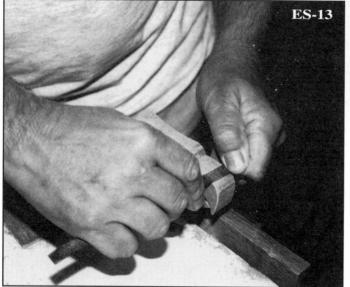

ES-13

ES-14

I want to get three dimensions into this piece right away. The beak plane has to go down substantially, so I take a riffler and just start to carve wood away. From the line in front of the eye, lower the beak plane considerably. After taking down the beak plane, I want to make a dramatic cut into the mouth area between the top and bottom of the beak. Just as was done in the Bellamy Eagle, I use a scroll saw after making a starter hole in the drill-press. Refer to Bellamy Eagle project for this step (photo ES-15).

After clamping your eagle's head in the bench vise, use a wood rasp to create a nice smooth radius on the edges of the head (photo ES-16 and ES-17).

ES-16

ES-15

ES-17

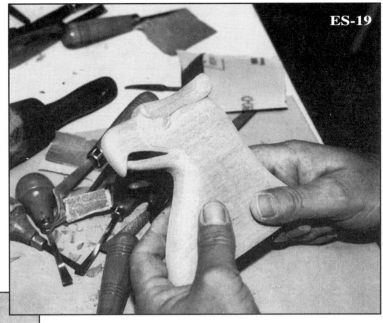

Refer often to the Bellamy Eagle project as you carve and shape the head to your satisfaction. Turn next to the shield. This piece will stay essentially the same size and will be the most geometrically linear of all of the components. However, it is not flat. The face has two planes meeting dead center that rise slightly from the outside edge to meet in the center. Refer to the photo of the completed Eagle for these details *(photo ES-18 and ES-19)*.

THE WINGS

Transfer just the top feather from your pattern to the board. Because the lower feathers would just be sanded off in the power sanding to follow *(photo ES-20)*.

ES-21

ES-22

As necessary, clamp the wing section to your bench to securely hold it while you shape the wing to the desired plane with your belt sander *(photos ES-21 through ES-23)*.

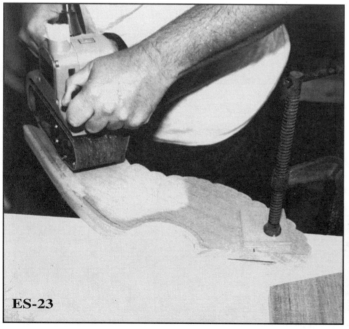

ES-23

After you have shaped and smoothed the wing using the belt sander, rifflers, and sandpaper as needed, place the pattern on the wing and draw on the lines for the rest of the feathers. Carve out the feathers, referring to the Bellamy Eagle as needed *(photos ES-24 through ES-28)*.

THE UPPER AND LOWER RIBBONS

Carve these as you would the Reliance nameboard. Refer to that section of this book as necessary. Refer to photo ES-1 to see how the project comes together.

COMPLETING THE PROJECT

At this point, all the components are carved and you are ready to glue it together.

Place a sheet of waxed paper on your bench. Wet the carving edges that are to be joined with a liberal amount of West Epoxy. Slide all the pieces together as you insert the biscuits or dowels.

ES-24

Simply hold the pieces firmly together and use several pieces of masking tape as your clamps. The West Epoxy doesn't have to be clamped very hard in order for it to work well.

After the epoxy has set, sand off the excess epoxy and finish the eagle as desired.

ES-25

ES-26

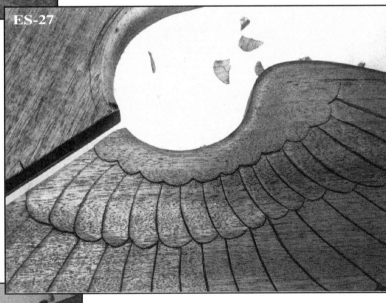

ES-27

ES-28

JAKE'S EAGLE

I named this Jake's Eagle after my young son saw it and decided he liked it enough to carry it in his stroller. It's a relatively small eagle, so that made it easy for him to hold. I borrowed this design from a 19th-century Polychrome eagle.

This is a complicated carving because it is made in one piece. There is a certain amount of fluidity that can only be carved. It also has to be done on a thick board for depth. I could have epoxied another board on top for the eagle's head and neck, but I

I've drawn on the major lines of the pattern as a cutting guide. I like to carve the head first as usual for the reasons I've already mentioned. It also will give you a feel for the various planes and a much better idea of how much meat to remove. I start to carve even before I've cut out the design. Using an assortment of hand tools, define the beak and neck areas. Then, cut out the bottom of the pattern with a bandsaw or sabre saw (photos JE-3 and JE-4).

thought it would be more interesting to have the luxury of so much original depth all the way across the design.

The smallness of the eagle that makes it so appealing to Jake brings some new carving challenges. Tools for work in this eagle must be super sharp. Also, it takes virtually every hand tool I own to carve this design. There are a lot of tight spaces.

I've chosen mahogany because the wood is a little softer than teak. While teak allows more carving detail, the mahogany allows me to remove large amounts of wood more quickly. If you break off a piece — such as the beak — just epoxy it back on. If you're going to gold leaf, little carving mistakes can be easily hidden.

The carving technique in Jake's Eagle is very similar to the Bellamy Eagle. There is nothing in the way of "building" though, in this project, so you can get to the carving nearly right away.

Jake's Eagle is attractive displayed in conjunction with a nameboard such as Reliance arched over the top with a reversed arched board for the hailport. I use Jake's Eagle as an integral part of the sign I use at trade shows (photo JE-1 and JE-2).

The next steps I show can be very dangerous if you are not very familiar with a table saw and bandsaw. Observe how I use the table saw to remove a large amount of wood. This cut removes enough wood so that the plane is as high as the highest feather under the eagle's neck (photos JE-5 through JE-8).

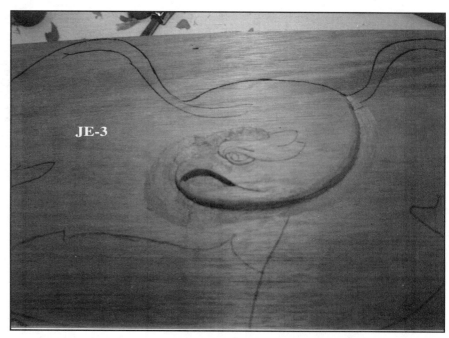

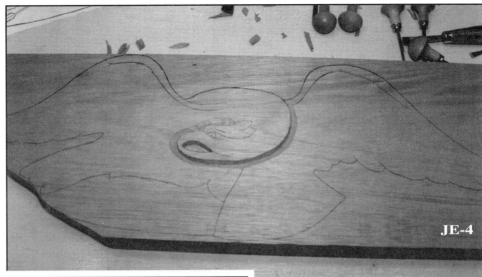

JE-4

JE-5

JE-6

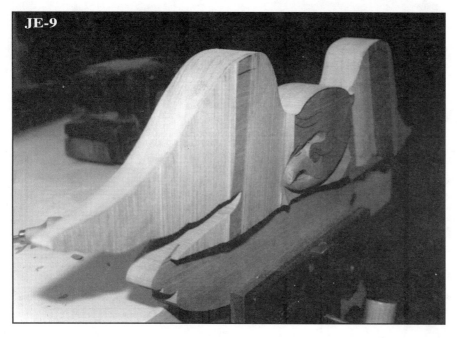

As you can observe in this photo, I have removed quite a lot of excess wood using my bandsaw. You could also accomplish this step by using a hand or power plane *(photo JE-9)*.

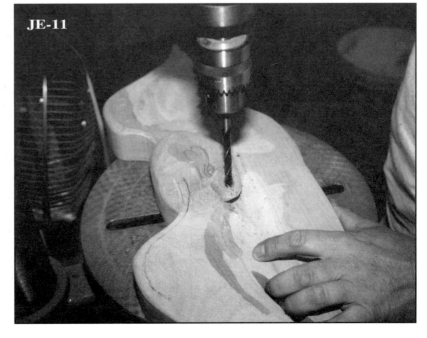

C-clamp the eagle to your bench. With an angle grinder fitted with a carbide disk or sanding pad with 36-grit paper, take away some wood under the arched ridges of the wings. You're looking for the same kind of depth you created at this point with the Bellamy Eagle (photos JE-10 and JE-10a).

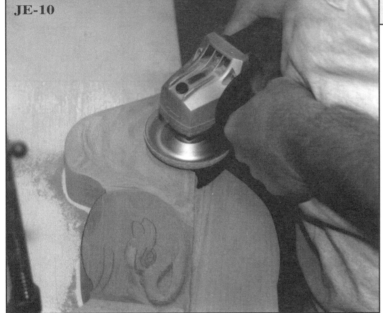

Put the eagle into your drillpress and bore a hole toward the front edge of the mouth. Be careful no to go too deeply (photo JE-11).

Continue to clear out wood under the head and the beak. Using an assortment of chisels and gouges, work across the grain or with the grain as the wood allows. Work on the table, put the eagle in the vise, come back to the table and return to the vise. Notice the following photographic sequence to understand the carving you're doing (*photos JE-12 through JE-23*).

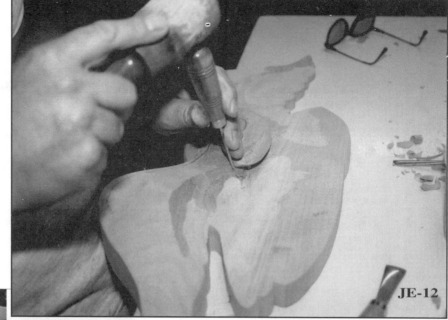

JE-12

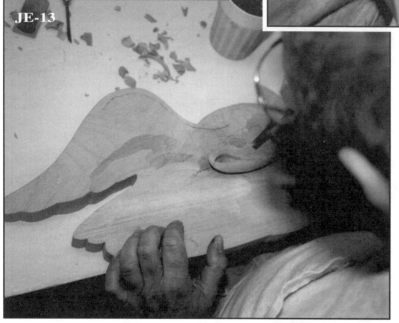

JE-13

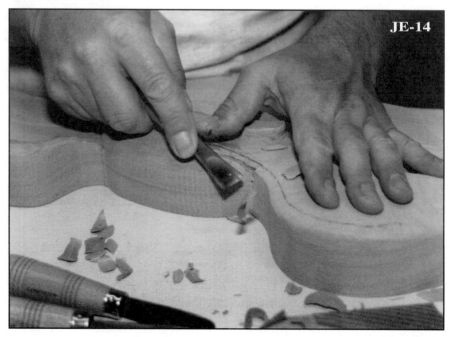

JE-14

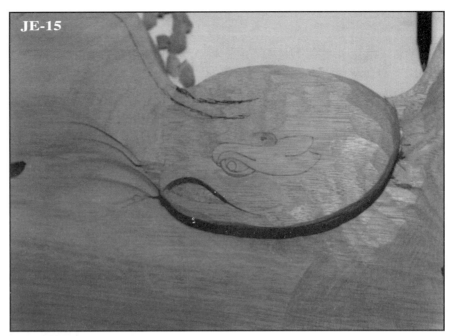

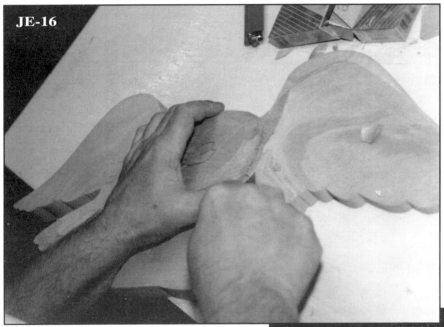

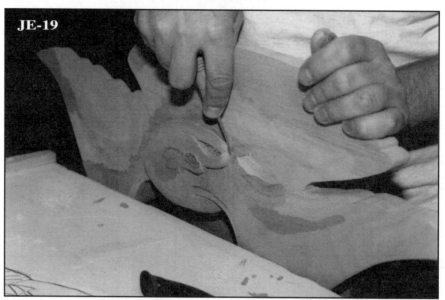

JE-21

JE-22

JE-23

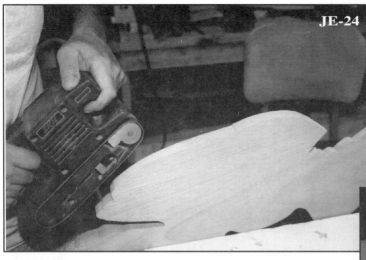

Use a beltsander to smooth out the edges and the plane of the shield, claws and arrows *(photos JE-24 and JE-25)*.

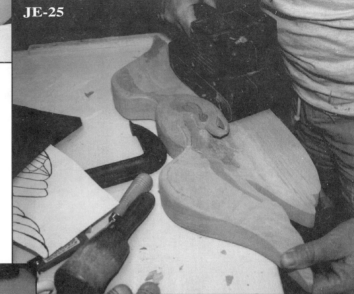

Place your template on this area of the eagle and trace in the claws only *(photos JE-26 and JE-27)*.

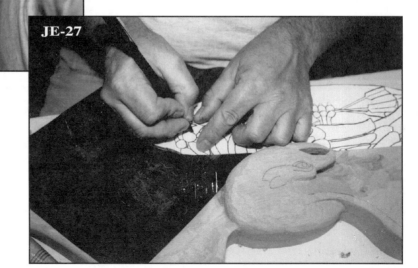

Rough carve the claws, lower the remaining area where the shield and arrows go, cut the claws out of the pattern and trace in the remaining details and carve them *(photos JE-28 and JE-29)*.

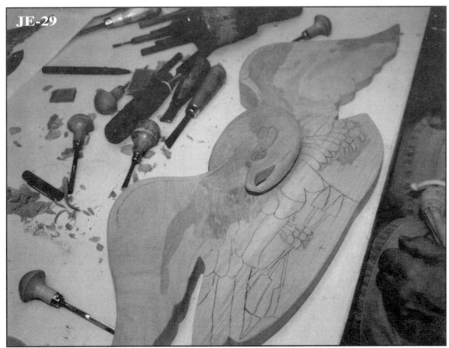

Shape the plane of the wings using power and hand tools as you did on the Bellamy Eagle *(photo JE-30)*.

JE-31

Cut your wing patterns so they fit nicely into the wings and trace on the feathers *(photo JE-31 and JE-31a).*

JE-31a

If you follow all the carving techniques you have mastered, use all the tools you own (and a few more you wish you had), you will have accomplished carving one of the most difficult and time consuming projects I have ever carved. You are now ready to finish and gold leaf.

CONGRATULATIONS!

CHAPTER 8

FINISHING: NAMEBOARDS AND EAGLES

Once you've completed all the steps involved in design, layout and carving, you're ready to apply a finish to your project. This is probably the most straightforward process in the entire book because you have to follow the rules to the letter. There is no creativity allowed in the application of paints and varnishes. Be extremely meticulous in every step of the finishing process and you'll have a long-lasting, beautiful project.

Safety should be number one in your thoughts. Pay serious attention to the caution labels on the chemicals involved and the directions for mixing. Make sure you have adequate ventilation because the petroleum-based chemicals are extremely toxic. A mask with a filter is recommended. And when you dispose of left-over varnish or thinner, think of the environment. I pour all my chemical waste on a plastic drop cloth and allow it to dry prior to disposal.

Your creativity in finishing comes through your choice of color, whether to varnish or paint. If you have a traditional project, you'll want to see the grain of the wood. A varnished finish will be best. A modern, sleek project may be better enhanced by a painted finish. Several finish types and colors are discussed here to give you an idea of your options, but you can find many more through paint charts and at your marine supply store.

The finishing systems I mention in this book are the ones I use. That isn't to say there aren't other equally good products, but my experience with West System Epoxy, Interlux Paints, and Clipper Varnish has been extremely durable in the marine environment.

I recommend you read this whole chapter before opening the first can or selecting the first brush. This is a long process that will require your attention for several days, so know what you're getting into before you start.

FINISHING-STEP BY STEP

After your nameboard is carved, cast a critical eye to smoothness of the entire surface. Begin final sanding by going over the surface with a beltsander with 80-grit sandpaper. Then, use a random orbital sander with 80-grit then 100-grit sandpaper.

All scratch marks must be removed. Get your nose down to the board and be very particular. If you miss a scratch, it's going to be very obvious —- and impossible to fix — once it is under the epoxy and varnish.

MATERIALS AND SUPPLIES:

West System Epoxy: 105 Resin with 207 Hardener
1 can Interlux Surfacing Putty #257
2 cans Clipper Varnish #95
    (Save one for the final coat)
Interlux Special Thinner 216 (For spray application)
Interlux Brushing Liquid 333 (For brush application)
Sandpaper for Beltsander, Vibrating Sander,
    & Random Orbital Sander in grits 80,120 & 220
Several disposable 1" bristle brushes
Several disposable 1", 2½", 3" foam brushes
Artist's brush
Supply of tack clothes
Disposable rags
Drying rack away from dust and air movement
Face mask with filters

Coat the front face of the board using West System Epoxy. I use 105 Resin and 207 Hardener. The 206 Hardener is for gluing. Mix them according to directions on the cans (*photo F-1*).

F-1

F-2a

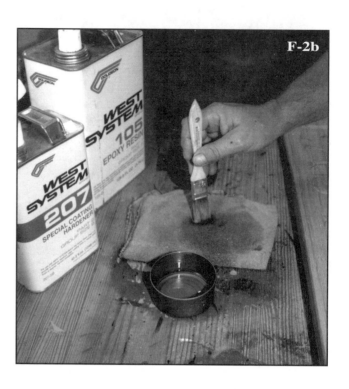

F-2b

Apply a very thin coat of this mixture using a 1" disposable bristle brush on all edges and the face of the board. Allow this coat to cure overnight. I thin the epoxy by dipping my brush into lacquer/epoxy thinner, touch it to a rag and then into the epoxy. If you use the epoxy without thinning it, it may cause a total failure of the finish if moisture gets under the epoxy. Thinning allows the epoxy to penetrate deeper into the wood (*photos F-2a through F-5*).

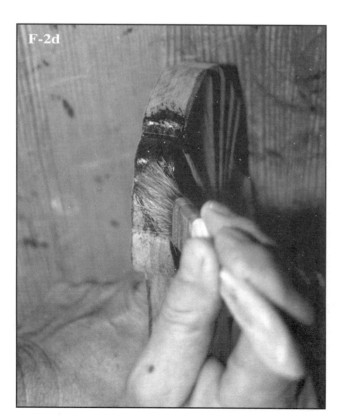

F-2d

F-2c

After the first coat of epoxy has cured, apply Interlux Surfacing Putty to any scratches or holes **INSIDE** the letters only. Use a stiff 1" putty knife to apply and smooth the putty.

Flip the board to the back side and apply the West System Epoxy to it. If you have drips down the edge, brush them away. Wait a day for this coat to cure.

Flip the board to the front. Take a small, folded square of 80-grit sandpaper and sand the letters smooth. If you're working on a scrolled or ribboned nameboard, lightly sand those areas with100-grit paper. Take your vibrating sander and lightly sand everything with 100-grit paper. Blow or vacuum the dust away and wipe it with a tack cloth. Be very cautious with the dust from sanding epoxy. Wear a mask and blow all dust outside.

Apply a second coat of West System Epoxy to the front side. Smooth it, being sure to pick out stray brush hairs. Let it cure for a day.

Flip the board to the back side, sand with 100-grit paper, and apply your second coat to it. You now have two full coats on the entire board. As usual, wait a day for it to cure.

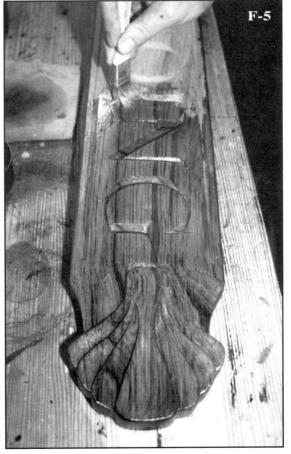

At this point, you have a decision. Will you brush or spray on your varnish. For the sake of continuity, I will continue with the choice to brush. Spraying is addressed at the end of this section. Make sure to blow or vacuum off all dust and then wipe the entire board with a tack cloth prior to every coat (*photo F-6*).

Take a bristle brush and dip it into Clipper Varnish. Jab the brush into letters and carved areas, and lay it smoothly on the front surface. I like to thin the varnish with a little 333 Interlux brushing liquid (*photos F-7a through F-9*).

F-8

Now this is going to get very repetitive, but it's important to work carefully. Repeat as many coats of Clipper Varnish to all surfaces — drying a day between sides and always taking care to sand with 220-grit sandpaper, then cleaning away the dust — until you can't see any glossy spots on the surface after sanding. Glossy spots mean you haven't done an ample job of complete coverage. You will have 4 to 6 coats of varnish on here before the final coat. Make sure to brush out letters and scrollwork with an artist's brush at every coat of varnish.

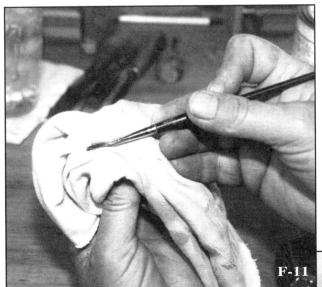

F-11

F-9

Clean out the letters and carved areas of excess varnish with an artist's brush, taking care to wipe the excess on a disposable cloth. Let it dry for the day (photos F-10 and F-11).

Sand everything with 220-grit sandpaper. Use a vibrating sander on the face of the front. Use a folded square for scroll work and inside the letters. Blow or vacuum the dust away. Wipe with a tack cloth.

F-10

BRUSHING ON THE FINAL COAT

If you've been very patient and meticulous to this point, you are close to completing a very successful finishing job.

After sanding with 220-grit paper, blow off the dust. Wipe the board with a brand new tack rag. You don't want to risk leaving even a particle of sanding dust on the board.

Always use a **NEW** can of Clipper Varnish for this last coat. You want a perfectly smooth product for this important last coat. Mix a small amount of brushing liquid into it — see the can for proportions — and take a 2½" bristle brush.

Apply varnish to the letters, scrollwork and edges first with your bristle brush. Then, do the surface in nice, even, flowing strokes. Brush out the excess from the letters and carving with an artist's brush. Wipe the brush frequently on a cloth.

F-12

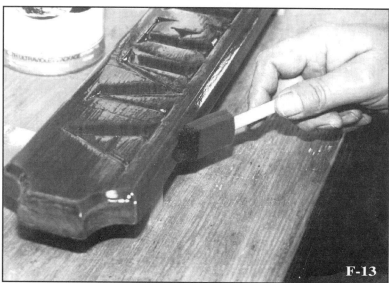

F-13

SPRAYING

Go back to the sentence about deciding to brush or spray. If you're going to spray, you will need an air compressor and spray gun (or an HVLP system like I use). Be sure to wear a mask and arrange a place outside where you can do the spraying.

Use Clipper Varnish but this time add Special Thinner 216 instead of the 333. With your nozzle from 12" to 18" away, spray all edges. Then, spray back and forth 3 or 4 times applying very thin coats (*photos F-14 and F-15*).

When everything is perfect, set aside to dry for a day or two in a dust-free place. CONGRATULATIONS! You've done it.

A helpful hint on doing the final coat of varnish is to take a 2½" to 3" foam brush, dampen it with varnish/brushing liquid mixture and carefully draw it across the face of the nameboard. This will remove brush marks and give you a better finish. Now, you can go ahead and brush out your letters and scrollwork with your artist's brush (*photo F-12*).

Don't forget to brush out the edges of the board with your foam brush. The finish on the top edge of the board is the most important because the varnish over time will deteriorate from that edge down (*photo F-13*).

F-14

Take the board inside to your shop bench. Dip a foam brush in varnish to slightly dampen it and brush out the drips on the edges. You have about 10 minutes to successfully do this. If your brush develops drag, dampen it slightly once more. Clean out the letters and carved areas with an artist's brush. Set aside to dry (photo F-16).

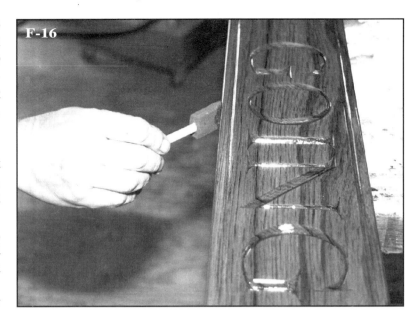

At this point, you're going to return to the first directions to continue the process of varnishing, drying, sanding, wiping, and varnishing until you have 4 to 6 coats on the nameboard.

When you are ready to spray on the final coat, sand carefully, clean the dust meticulously and spray a thick coat on the edges and 4 to 6 very thin continuous coats on the surface.

This fairly heavy coating will help drown any dust particles and give you a spectacular final coat.

Carefully bring the board in from outside and brush out the letters and scrollwork. Brush out the edges with a foam brush only. Set the board aside in a dust-free area for two to three days prior to gold leafing.

A painted finish is achieved in exactly the same way as a varnish finish except that you choose your favorite color of Interlux Brightside Polyurethane and apply it in the same manner described for the varnish. One other exception is that the amount of paint applied at each coat will be slightly less than the corresponding amount of varnish.

If you have chosen a very dark color like black, blue or green, you can coat the painted finish with the Clipper varnish and have a higher gloss and a finish that's easier to maintain.

Speaking about maintenance, here's what I suggest: Your painted or varnished nameboard is going to deterio-

rate from the edges first, but you can delay the deterioration of the face of the board by maintaining the edges. Several times a year, lightly sand the edges of the nameboard with 220-grit sandpaper and apply several coats of new finish with a 1" foam brush, taking care not to touch the boat or the face of the board. Remember — the UV light of the sun is what causes the deterioration of a marine finish. If you live in a high UV area, recoat more often. A sure sign that recoating is necessary is a loss of gloss on your finish.

TWO-PART POLYURETHANE FINISHES

There are advantages and disadvantages to these super hard, high gloss finishes (photo F-17 and F-18).

The advantages are extremely high gloss compared to one-part varnish or paint. A very hard surface that seems to be impervious to almost anything and will last two to three times longer than one-part finish.

The disadvantages are the same. The very high gloss may take away from the warm look of teak or mahogany that traditional one-part finishes create. The very hard surface, once it has finally deteriorated, can be almost impossible to remove when a complete refinish becomes necessary.

The extra expense of purchasing these products makes the cost ratio the same, as if you refinish with one-part finishes two to three times.

I am personally most familiar with two brands of these modern finishes. Awl-Grip, made by U.S. Paint, and Interthane Plus, made by Interlux. I only spray these, so if you intend to apply them by brush, see the manufacturer's instructions.

F-17

wear a long-sleeved shirt, long pants and even disposable painter's suit to cover yourself as much as possible when mixing, applying or sanding. The smell of these chemicals is fairly pungent, so be considerate of your neighbors when you're applying it.

So far, it sounds pretty dangerous. *Well, it is.*

After carefully mixing the polyurethane in a separate container, spray a small amount of the proper thinner through your spray gun. This will help eliminate any possibility of a chemical reaction. Mix only the amount you intend to use because it can't be saved after mixing.

Pour the mixture into your spray gun and apply a tack coat — very thin — to the carefully sanded and cleaned nameboard. Wait several minutes. Apply a

Awl-Grip and Interthane Plus are very similar in methods and characteristics of application, so I will describe a typical application in a nameboard.

DAVE'S DISCLAIMER

This isn't intended to be a manual for the application of two-part polyurethane finishes. That would require a complete book on just this subject. My intention is to just introduce you to the existence of these finishes and to share my own experience with them

Consult the instructions supplied with the brands you choose and do not deviate from them. Consult the manufacturer with any questions.

A NOTE: Interthane Plus comes with an audio tape in the package to instruct you on proper mixture and application. Read the instructions on the Awl-Grip label.

As with one-part finishes, I seal the wood with West System Epoxy, but I use three coats on the face. This allows all of the grain to be filled. These finishes, when properly thinned for spraying, are almost like water in their consistency, so they don't fill the grain well.

I mix my finishes exactly as described on the label. Never deviate from the manufacturer's instruction or you may suffer a chemical reaction that will cause a huge mess. Remember, these chemicals require a mixture of polyurethane, catalyst and thinner. In some circumstances, they include a fast-cure accelerator, inhibited-cure accelerator or flattening agent. It will also be necessary to use tack rags that are chemically compatible with these products. These products can cause injury to you through contact with the skin or breathing either the products themselves or the dust released into the air during sanding.

Always use a chemical-rated respirator while mixing, applying or sanding these products. I also recommend you

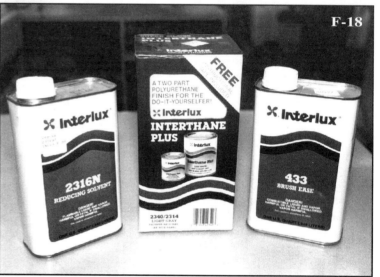

F-18

wet coat. Your coats of two-part polyurethane should be much thinner than if you were applying a one-part varnish. These brands of polyurethane indicate that you may apply additional coats within 24 hours and still have chemical adhesion. I have never tried doing this because I believe in sanding between coats of any finish to achieve the "flatness" necessary for a quality appearance. I have discovered that 2 or 3 coats of build-up is more than adequate prior to the final coat.

Basically, follow all procedures for brushing out the letters and eagles as described in the one-part section. For the final coat, I don't advise "flooding out the dust" as you can with Clipper Varnish. A very heavy coat of two-part will cause problems you don't even want to know about. I sometimes use a fast-cure accelerator for the final coat because it doesn't seem to affect the durability of the finish and it dries so quickly that less airborne dust settles into it. Also, I always use clear over any color for the final coat. It aids in maintenance in that you can touch up the edges with less mess and clear appears to have more gloss than the colors.

CHAPTER 9
GOLD LEAFING

The rich patina of gold on a nameboard or eagle is the element that sets it apart from others that are simply varnished or painted. The shimmering effect of gold leafing in carved letters on a nameboard creates a sense of richness you can't create with gold paint. Only pure gold can lend a special quality to your project.

There is a lot of unnecessary mystery surrounding gold leafing. People who haven't done it tend to shy away from the idea of trying to learn the technique because it sounds difficult and it seems to be very expensive.

Of all the phases involved in any project in my shop, the application of gold leaf into a carved letter is probably one of my favorites. It is one of the easiest applications to do, so "gold leaf days" are fun. It requires reasonable care to do well, but serious mistakes won't happen if you pay attention to the very basic rules of application. You're going to be pleasantly surprised at how easy it is to become an expert.

As with everything else in this book, I taught myself this technique. My process may vary from the way traditionalists work, but this has worked well for me and my clients. After 25 years of doing work for clients on a repeat basis, I know my leafing has held up to the rigors of the marine environment.

Despite the seemingly fragile nature of gold leaf in the thin sheets — much thinner than paper — it is a hardy substance that holds up to all kinds of weather for years. Gold leaf actually reflects UV light. When it is used in a carved letter, it is never varnished over because that would dull the luster and diminish the effect. Even applied to a nameboard on a transom where water is likely to splash regularly, you can count on gold leaf to remain beautiful for years.

Before I start to explain the process of applying gold leaf, it would be good for you to know something about the material from an expert. Mr. Arnold A. Jacobs of Art Essentials of New York, Ltd . — my favorite leaf supplier — was kind enough to send some information about the different types of gold and silver leaf available.

The technical differences between products of the same description from different national origins are more a matter of taste and standard color.

Surface leaf is the thinnest suitable for gilding of opaque surfaces (wood, metal or plastic). Glass leaf is used for reverse glass gilding, it is not cloudy when held against light and has less pinholes. Double leaf is heavier, triple is heavier yet. Differences of the various thickness is 10-15% over the lower grade. This is completely without influence on handling and application. Heavier grades tend to have special qualities (glass) or have more substance for agate burnishing.

The silver look is available with aluminum, white gold and platinum leaf. For carved letters, surface leaf is sufficiently heavy and is more economical than other grades and more brilliant than Patent leaf. Patent leaf is more convenient to use for those unskilled in gilding with surface leaf and it costs more, while being less brilliant. German patent is looser on paper, Italian patent is suitable for high wind conditions also. Eagle gilding is substantially the same as carved sign gilding.

18K is lemon gold, 16.7K is pale gold, 12K is white gold, 22K is interior grade yellow gold, 23K is exterior grade yellow gold and 24K is 100% pure gold.

Arnold A. Jacobs
Art Essentials of New York, Ltd.
1-800-283-5323

letters, 16 to 20 sheets should do the job nicely for each nameboard.

I would caution you to avoid being cheap with gold. If you've worked to carry a special project this far, it would be a shame to find yourself not applying a sufficient amount of leaf to do the project correctly.

APPLYING GOLD LEAF

There are three distinct steps in gold leafing. After your project is completely varnished, you will lay down a wet medium called "size" in the carved letter that will create the adhesive surface for your gold. When this is properly tacky, you'll lay down the gold. Finally, after you've done a good job getting the gold in place, you'll outline the work.

SIZE

I have had great results with my own leafing size. It is a mixture of 60% One Shot Imitation Gold Paint and 40% Quick Dry Gold Leaf Size.

Think of size as a kind of landing pad for your gold leaf. This surface will create a tight bond between the leaf and the board. You need to apply the size smoothly and evenly, avoiding standing puddles in the bottoms of your letters, and not spilling over too far onto the uncarved surface of the board. The neatness with which you apply the size will have a direct impact on how the gold looks when you're through.

This process, once begun, cannot be stopped.

THE SIZE: MATERIALS AND SUPPLIES

You will need the following for applying the size and gold leafing the project (*photo GL-1*):

One Shot Imitation Gold Paint
Quick Dry Gold Leaf Size
Disposable Painter's Filters
Jar for mixing
a small linoleum block
#5 sable artist's brush (Grumbacher Beaux Arts 190 Series Red Sable is what I use.)
#10 and #12 Simmons #88 Camel Hair Brushes
100% Cotton Balls
Baby Powder
Surface Gold Leaf (Italian and Japanese shown)

Pour the One Shot into a jar. If it's a new can, you can use it straight from the can. If you've used it before and a skin has formed, lift off the skin and discard it. Filter your paint through a disposable painter's filter

You may need to read this information each time you set out to do a leafing project, but I'll share my preferences with you.

I prefer to use 23K Italian surface gold leaf because, as delicate as the sheets are, the Italian books tend to hold together better than the Japanese ones. To tell the truth, I find the Japanese leaf terribly messy because the books are not bound together and you have to deal with loose tissue paper and gold leaf. It is too easy to ruin a sheet if your aim is off or someone causes a sudden breeze nearby. Probably the best application for Japanese leaf is on an eagle carving, or carved nameboard end, where you just want to lay down a whole bunch of gold. However, it is a very good value for gold leaf coverage and I use it a lot.

I use surface leaf because it is relatively economical. The pinholes don't matter at all. Although my primary leaf is gold, I've found a few opportunities to use a silver look, but I don't use actual silver because it tarnishes. Platinum or aluminum are better choices for the marine environment. The aluminum leaf should always be covered with a clear varnish — a step never taken with 23K gold leaf in a carved letter.

THE COST

Gold is not a small investment, but it isn't outrageous. Italian books include 25 sheets. I buy a pack of books — or 20 books at a time — so I always have 500 leaves available to me. Of course, you don't need to maintain that large a supply if you aren't in business doing this work. Your needs as a hobbyist will vary based upon the size of your project. In order to calculate, figure you'll need up to two sheets (with a few crumbs left over) to fill an average 4-inch high letter. If your boat has 8

available at any paint or hardware store. Mix in the Gold Leaf Size at a ratio of 60/40 respectively. You should have a creamy texture. In fact, it should look and move a lot like heavy cream. If it is too thin, add more paint. Too thick, add more size.

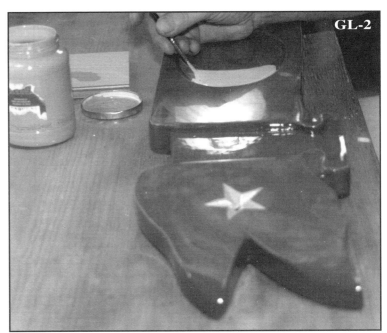

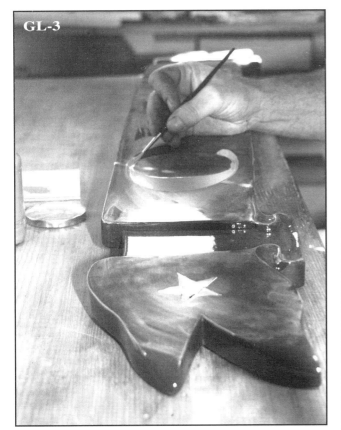

Dip your sable brush into the jar and carry some of the mixture to the linoleum block — your artist's palette — and work it there with your brush. Carry the mixture

from the palette to the carved letter and paint a smooth, drip-free coat in the carved area. I am counting on your hand-eye coordination abilities for doing this reasonably well. Stay within the carving as much as possible. Use the point of the brush to move from the inside to the outside for serifs or corners of letters. Watch for puddles and brush them out.

If you accidentally slip to the outside of a letter, it will probably be covered in the outlining step. If you get distracted and make a big mistake, you can take a cotton rag moistened with mineral spirits and run it quickly over the spot to remove it. I don't recommend putting yourself in this position, so be careful. Any pause and correction is going to create potential problems because the size is beginning to dry. If your error is not large, leave it alone *(photos GL-2 through GL-5)*.

Keep a sharp eye to the inside of the carved letter, too, being sure you haven't missed a spot. If there is no size, the gold won't stick. As I said in the workshop chapter, good lighting is essential all the way through. Be careful stray brush hairs don't stick in the size. These will cause unattractive ridges if they are allowed to dry.

A trick I've learned is to create a minor ridge of size just at the surface all the way around the carved letter. This will be a helpful guide for the outlining step *(photo GL-6)*.

GL-6

When you put a new brush load of size on your palette, stay out of the old one. It is already drying and there's a chance you might drag a few loose bristles from the brush. When you have finished, clean your brush. These brushes aren't cheap and they bear some consideration if you don't plan to spend a fortune on replacements. Clean them with a lacquer thinner and store them **FLAT** in a closed container filled with Neetsfoot Oil.

Put the board on a drying rack or in some location away from dust and disturbance. Since I have projects in various phases in my shop all the time, I have a large exhaust fan installed in the wall. It pulls shop dust away from the drying racks. Still, I don't do sanding when I am drying size in the shop.

Wait for about 1 to 1½ hours and, toward the end of the drying time; touch it with your knuckle rather than your fingertip. When it is tacky and makes a slight snap, it is time to apply the gold. You can't

put it off. Once again, block out time for yourself and don't stop. Refer to Gold leafing a Carved Nameboard End or Eagle for a photo of using your knuckle.

WHY THE GOLD MUST WAIT TILL THE SIZE SAYS IT'S TIME

The reason you can't wait to apply the gold leaf to the size it this: if the size is too wet, the gold will be dull; if the size is too dry, the gold leaf won't stick.

If this is your first time using size and gold leafing, you may want to apply the size to a scrap board when you apply it to your project. You can test a small amount of the gold on the scrap. It's a small sacrifice for peace of mind.

APPLYING GOLD LEAF TO LETTERS

Place your board on your workbench and get comfortable. Be sure you are in a breeze-free area and that no one will interrupt you until you have finished applying the gold.

Take a book of gold leaf in one hand, open it to a sheet, move the book to the vicinity of the first letter — I prefer working left to right in most situations — and gently lift the sheet with your brush to position it inside the carved letter. Slide it carefully and, once in the letter, lift the edges that overlap onto the board's surface, and fold it back into the carved area. Be careful to transfer the sheet as intact as possible into the letter *(photo GL-7)*.

GL-7

GL-8

GL-9

Take your brush and push the leaf into place, taking **_GREAT_** care not to touch the exposed size with the brush. There must always be gold between the brush and the size. With a rapid and soft feathering motion "paint" the gold into place very gently, adding more gold as necessary. You will generate a lot of crumbs, but these can be scooted into the corner of the next letter. Use this excess dust in the serifs — not in the wide parts of the letters (*photos GL-8, GL-9 and GL-10*).

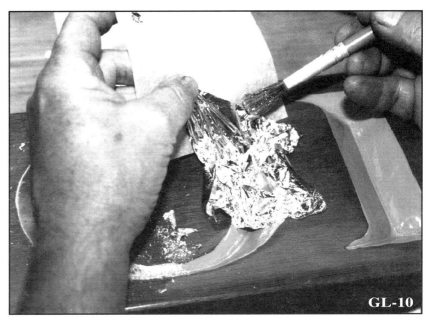

GL-10

GL-11

Clean the board by vacuuming or blowing away all of the dust and excess powder. Take a 100% cotton rag — an old T-shirt is ideal — and dampen the end of one finger wrapped in the rag in 100% mineral spirits. Carefully rub the surface of the board without touching the letters. Immediately take a dry rag and rapidly move it around to polish the surface, still avoiding the letters. (I can only recommend using the mineral spirits on Interlux products and Awl-Grip. I have not tested this on other products to check for chemical reaction.) *(photos GL-12 and GL-13).*

Now, it's magic time. As you brush the gold, it begins to take on its first level of shine. Each light stroke of the brush smooths it even more. When you have finished your first letter, move on and repeat this process until you are through with all of the letters. With the remaining dust, go back over the letters with a very rapid and soft brushing stroke.

Allow about 24 hours to pass, then take a 100% cotton ball in your fingers and polish the gold in every nook and cranny. Excess powder may create a residue on the balls that will cause a drag, so discard it and use another one if this happens. Cotton balls are cheap! You are using mild, steady pressure, following the direction of the letters as you rub. If it feels crusty, just apply a little more pressure. You are now burnishing the gold *(photo GL-11).*

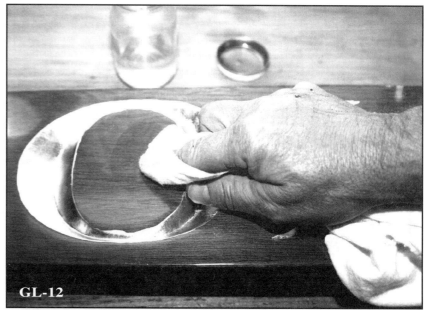
GL-12

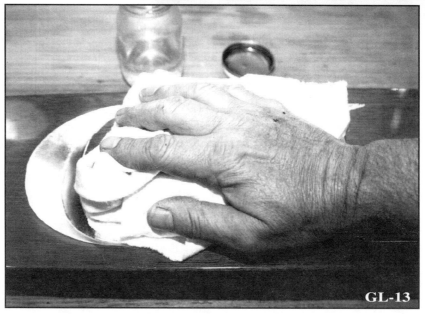
GL-13

GOLD LEAFING A CARVED NAMEBOARD END OR AN EAGLE

Now, you're going to have some real fun. This is beyond a doubt my favorite project in the shop. You've done a huge amount of work to this point carving and finishing your nameboard or eagle. (Finish an eagle the same as a varnished nameboard prior to this gold leafing stage.) You've come to the step that will be the easiest to do, but will show the most dramatic results.

Apply the size, carefully, to the area to be gold leafed. Be sure to cover the area completely *(photos GL-14 and GL-15)*.

Set the project aside and allow it to dry so that when you lightly place your knuckle on the size, you will feel a "snap" as you pull it off *(photo GL-16)*.

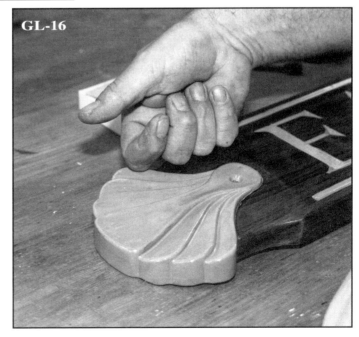

GL-17

GL-18

With the sheet of gold leaf in hand, still on the tissue paper, catch the leaf on the bottom edge and then flop it over onto the face *(photos GL-17 and GL-18)*.

Now proceed to apply a very liberal amount of gold onto the rest of the edges, as shown before, and on the face of the project. Keep the gold as flat as possible and gently push it down on all areas *(photos GL-19 through GL-21)*.

GL-19

Gold Leafing

GL-20

GL-21

After you have applied this liberal amount of gold leaf, use your #12 brush and, moving it in a light but very rapid motion, go over the entire area over and over again *(photos GL-22 and GL-23)*.

GL-22

GL-23

°GL-24

After allowing the size underneath to dry for at least 24 hours, use a wad of 100% cotton balls to burnish the gold. Be very careful not to scratch the gold leaf with a finger nail *(photo GL-24)*.

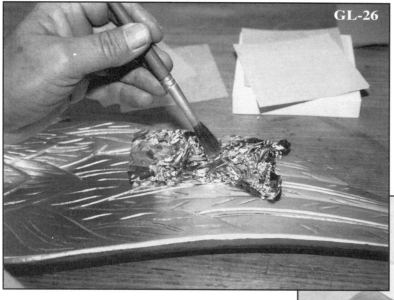

GL-26

As you can see in these photographs, gold leafing an eagle is exactly the same process *(photos GL-25 and GL-26)*.

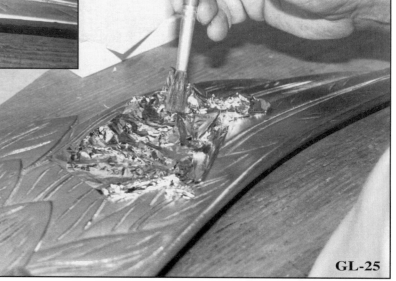

GL-25

GL-27

GOLD LEAFING FASTENINGS

If you have a gold leafed star or any other gold ornamentation on the ends of your nameboards, you can hide the screw or bolt heads very well by gold leafing them. (All holes should have been drilled prior to the finishing stage.) *(photo GL-27).*

Pre-paint the head of the fastener prior to applying the size. Then just paint on the size being sure that it's inside of the screwdriver slots *(photo GL-28).*

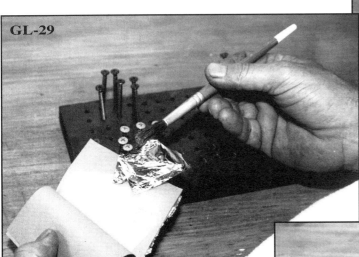

GL-29

GL-28

After allowing the size to dry properly, apply the leaf to the screw head *(photo GL-29).*

Then, using your #10 brush, push the gold into the slots and, rapidly moving the brush, cover the entire head of the fastener with leaf *(photo GL-30).*

GL-30

CHAPTER 10
OUTLINING NAMEBOARDS

This final step is somewhat tedious, but it makes all the difference between a professional-looking board and an amateur one. You'll be defining the brilliant gold and creating a sharp border between it and the varnished or painted board. This step will bring your work into focus.

MATERIALS AND SUPPLIES:

Grumbacher red sable 7357 #1 artist's brush
One Shot Paint, small can, or Interlux Brightside Polyurethane, black or coordinating color
Linoleum block for palette
(photo OT-1).

First, wash your hands, then sprinkle on a little baby powder. This will help your hands slide easier as you outline. Put a clean linoleum block in front of you and dip your brush into the jar of paint, carrying some to the block or palette. Take a deep breath and relax. I've done this work for so long that I actually enjoy outlin-

ing, but I remember the first time I did it. Just remember you're only going to get comfortable with outlining if you do it. The more you do it, the higher your confidence level will be, and the better your work will look.

OT-1

Outlining is a piecemeal activity. Concentrate on each letter as if it is the only one and address one line — or part of a line — at a time. If you rush ahead, you'll get your hands in the paint and make a terrible mess. Go slowly. This is a time to let your brain do its best thinking. There are only two different ways you will hold a brush for all outlining steps: one for pulling the brush towards you and the other for pulling it away.

This series of photographs will give you a good perspective because I'm doing a round letter and then a straight letter.

After you have thoroughly "brushed out" on the palette, hold the brush as shown and, starting at a comfortable spot, pull the brush in an arch away from you *(photo OT-2).*

OT-2

After you have followed that arch as far as you can comfortably go, add paint, and holding the brush as shown, pull the brush back towards you *(photo OT-3)*.

Using the first brushing method, do the inside of the letter, then, finish off the top arch as shown *(photo OT-4)*.

Complete outlining the "O" using the two methods of holding the brush.

A straight letter can be more difficult than a round one. A straight line is the hardest to draw or paint, freehand.

Holding the brush as shown, start at the point of the serif. Pull it around the curve, and then up the letter about halfway. (You'll need to add more paint before you can finish the letter.) *(photo OT-5)*.

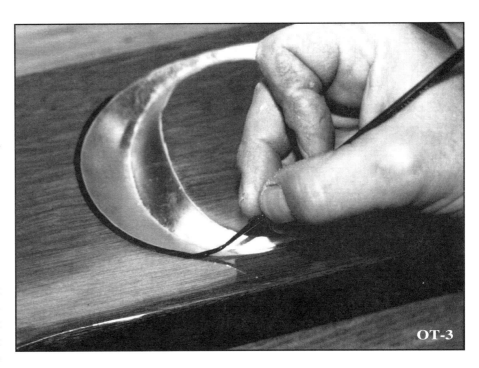

OT-3

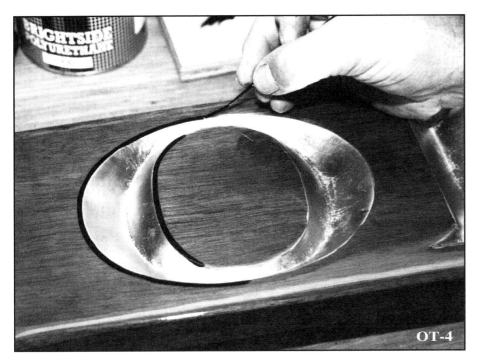

OT-4

After adding more paint to your brush, overlap the line where you left off and finish the straight line. Don't try to paint the outline in a curve away from you. The angle of the curve of the serif is too severe to attempt to finish while holding the brush this way. Simply add more paint and use the other hand position. Start at the top of the serif and paint towards the straight line *(photo OT-6)*.

Add paint to your brush and using this way of holding the brush, paint the top line *(photo OT-7)*.

You are actually able to paint the vertical lines using either brush holding method. Try them both and see what suits you the best. Remember, every time you finish painting a stroke of the letter, dip your brush in fresh paint and brush it out on your palette. Practice outlining as often as possible if you want to achieve professional results.

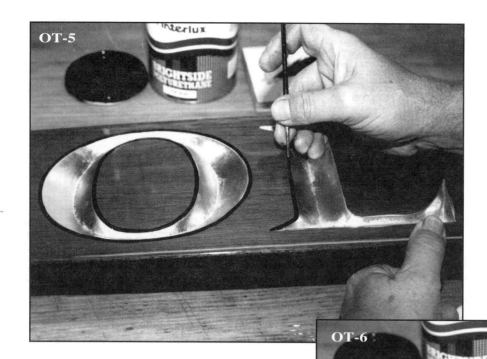

OT-5

OT-6

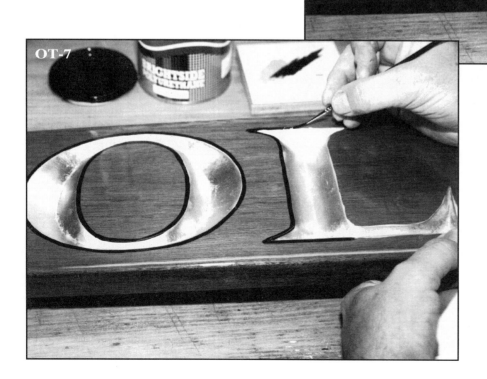

OT-7

APPENDIX

SAFETY TIPS

Have at your disposal, a chemical rated respirator, disposable dust masks, safety goggles with side shields and disposable gloves.

Let's start with the goggles with side shields. I wear glasses but there have been many occasions when I failed to wear my goggles over my glasses that I have had an eye injury. This most often occurs at the table saw or when using the router. These tools eject wood chips at a *very high velocity* and they bounce off your checks into the inside of your glasses and then bounce into your eye. Trust me on this one.

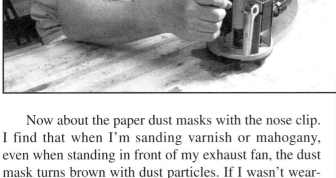

Now about the paper dust masks with the nose clip. I find that when I'm sanding varnish or mahogany, even when standing in front of my exhaust fan, the dust mask turns brown with dust particles. If I wasn't wearing the mask, all that dust would be in my lungs.

The chemical-rated respirator is the most important item in your shop. When you sand epoxy or two-part polyurethanes, the dust is very toxic and a paper mask doesn't fit tight enough to your face to protect you. Additionally, when spraying any type of paint or varnish, the air around you is full of vapors that are very hazardous to your health. You not only need the tight

fitting mask but you need the charcoal filter for protection from these vapors.

When dealing with paints and thinners, especially two-part polyurethanes, you need to wear gloves because these chemicals will enter your body through your pores.

Additionally, when I spray finishes, I wear long pants, a long sleeve shirt and my goggles with side shields. When I have finished my spraying, I shed these clothes, wash them and immediately take a shower. Don't fail to do this — you will regret the consequences.

LIST OF CARVING TOOLS
I USE FOR THE MAJORITY
OF MY CARVINGS:

3/4", 1", 1¼", AND 1½" Modified Butt Chisels
 (from hardware store)

General Tools Mfg. Co.
Six piece carving tool set #1293
(Buy this set for the 5/16" Bent Square Chisel)

Brienz Carving Mallet
Woodcraft Company Catalog #08G08

Swiss Palm-handled Carving Tools
6MM #7 Gouge 05Y42
5MM #9 Gouge 05Y62
8MM #5 Gouge 05X11
6MM #7 Gouge 05Y42
8MM Skew   05R09

Stubby Carving Tools
1/2" #5 Gouge   14I26
3/4" #3 Gouge   08W31
1/2" Chisel   08Z22

Dockyard Micro Carving Tools:
Micro Gouge Set 17N50
Micro Dogleg Chisel Set 17N60

Rifflers as you desire:
Woodcraft Company
210 Wood County Industrial Park
P.O. Box 1686
Parkersburg, West Virginia 26102-1686
1-800-535-4482

COMPLETE WOODCRAFT SETS OF CARVING
TOOLS I OWN AND USE:

Palm-handled Carving Set 05Y70

Pfeil "Swiss Made" Carving Tools (Long Handles)
#5 20MM Bent Gouge   05S08
#5 14MM Fishtail Gouge 05M09
 #5 20MM Fishtail Gouge 05M13
 #7 20MM Fishtail Gouge 05M14

Stubby Carving Tools
 Set of 8   09H90
Additional set of 4   14I25
Marples Bench Chisels
1/2"   12G41
3/4"   12G61
1"   12G71
1 1 /4" 12G81

ADDITIONAL WOODCRAFT ITEMS I OWN AND
FIND VERY USEFUL AROUND THE SHOP:

Honing Guide 03A21
Tapered Round Slipstones   07E02
Combination Coarse India/Fine India Stone   01W52
Hard Black Arkansas Stone   07O04
Leather Power Strop   08R31
Carbide Grinding Wheel   04D27
Combination Square Four Piece Set   14L90
12" Sliding Bevel Square   15R51
French Curve Set   01P11
Loose Wing Divider, 6"   06C21
Jorgensen 12" Rapid-Acting Vise   16T52
Portable Carver's Vise   01D10
Clamp'n Tool Guide, 36"   25L22
Improved Dowl-It   09Q51
Leather Shop Apron   03D52

Carbide Router Bits:
Round Over 1/8"R, 1/4" SH 24B92
Round Over 1/4"R, 1/4" SH 24B94
Round Over 3/8"R, 1/4" SH 24B96
Round Over 1/2"R, 1/4" SH 24B97
Champering 5/8", 1/4" SH   24L08
3/4" X 1/4" SH Carbide Mortising Bit

Power Tools I Use and Recommend
Reliant 20MM Drill Press
Reliant 16" Wood Band Saw
Reliant 12" Planer
Reliant 18" Scroll Saw

Powermatic Model 66-10" Table Saw
  with T-Square Fence System
DeWalt 12" Compound Mitre Saw DW705
DeWalt 1/2" VSR Drill   DW111
DeWalt 7 1/4" Circular Saw   DW364
Black and Decker 1 1/2HP Router 7614,
  Type 3, Dual Handled (If you have one router,
  this is it)
 Black and Decker Hand Planer ELU 3375

Porter Cable:
Model 555 Plate Joiner (Biscuit)
Model 505 1/2 Sheet Sander
Model 330 1/4 Sheet Sander
Model 352 VS-3" X 21" Belt Sander
Model 334 5" Random Orbit Sander
Model 7335 5" Variable Speed Random Orbit Sander
Model 7549 Top Grip Jig Saw
Model 6902 Heavy Duty Router
Model 7301 Laminate Trimmer
Model 7405 5" Angle Grinder
Model 666 EHD 3/8" Drill

TOOL & SUPPLY SOURCES I USE & RECOMMEND

Woodcraft Company
210 Wood County Industrial Park
P.O. Box 1686
Parkersburg, West Virginia 26102-1686
1-800-225-1153

Trend-Lines
135 American Legion Highway
Revere, Massachusetts 02151
1-800-877-7899

Woodworkers Supply, Inc.
1108 North Glenn Road
Casper, Wyoming 82601
1-800-645-9292

Gold Leaf
Art Essentials of New York, Ltd.
3 Cross Street
Suffern, New York 10901
1-800-283-5323

COMPUTER GENERATED LETTERING LAYOUT SOURCES I RECOMMEND

Computerized Lettering
1530 North Federal Highway
Pompano Beach, Florida 33062
1-800-321-5387

Fast Signs
4512 Oleander Drive
Wilmington, North Carolina 28403
1-800-909-SIGN

MY RECOMMENDED HARDWOOD SOURCES:

Anchor Hardwoods Company
6014-R Oleander Drive
Wilmington, North Carolina 28403
(910) 392-9888

Maritime Wood Products
Teak Connection
3361 SE Dixie Highway
Stuart, Florida 34997
1-800-274-8325

M.L. Condon Company, Inc.
260 Ferris Avenue
White Plains, New York 10603
(914) 946-4111

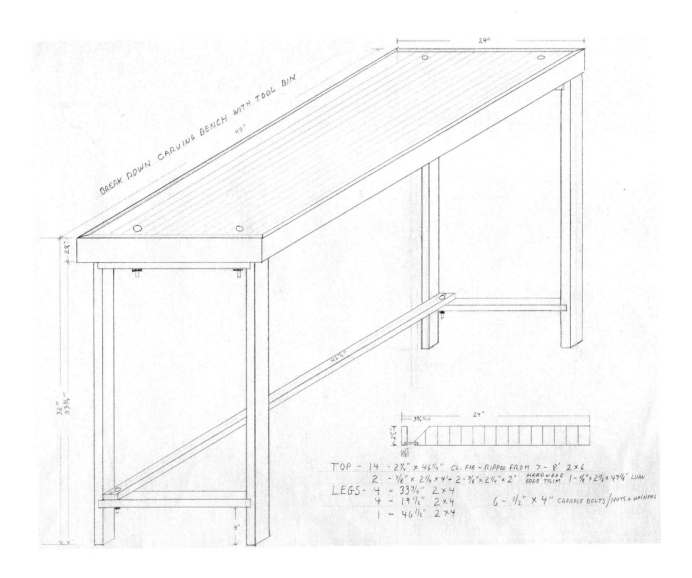

BREAK DOWN CARVING BENCH WITH TOOL BIN

24"

48"

24"

36"
33¾"

8"

3½"
2¼"
⅞"

24"

TOP - 14 - 2¼" × 46¼" CL. FIR - RIPPED FROM 7 - 8' 2×6
2 - ⅞" × 2¼ × 4' + 2 - ⅞" × 2¼" × 2'   HARDWOOD   1 - ⅛" × 2½ × 47¼" LUAN
EDGE TRIM
LEGS- 4 - 33¾" 2×4
4 - 19½" 2×4   6 - ½" × 4" CARRAGE BOLTS/NUTS + WASHERS
1 - 46½" 2×4

WORKBENCH   SEE FOLD-OUT PAGES FOR LARGE VERSION

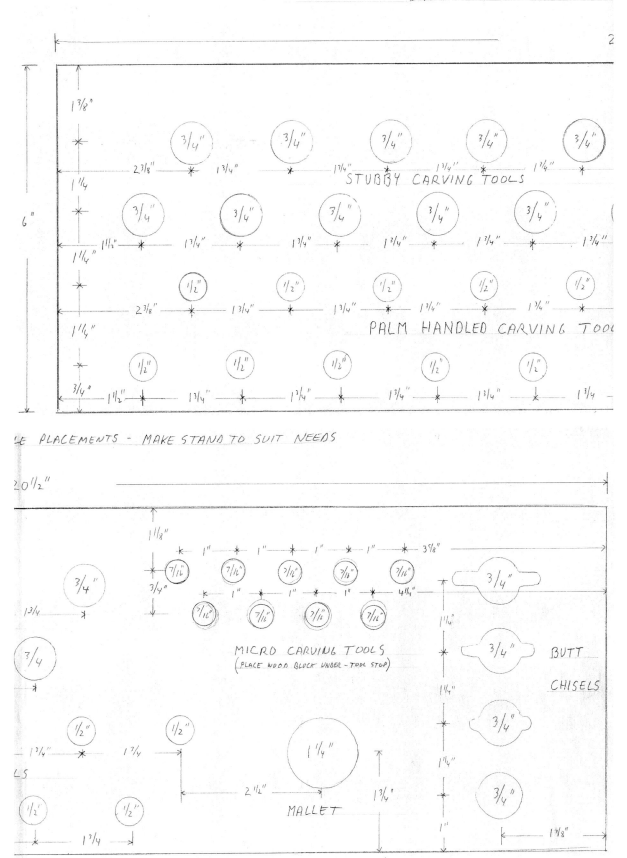

STUBBY CARVING TOOLS

PALM HANDLED CARVING TOOL

LE PLACEMENTS - MAKE STAND TO SUIT NEEDS

MICRO CARVING TOOLS
(PLACE WOOD BLOCK UNDER - TOOL STOP)

MALLET

BUTT

CHISELS

TOOL ORGANIZATION CHART   SEE FOLD-OUT PAGES FOR LARGE VERSION

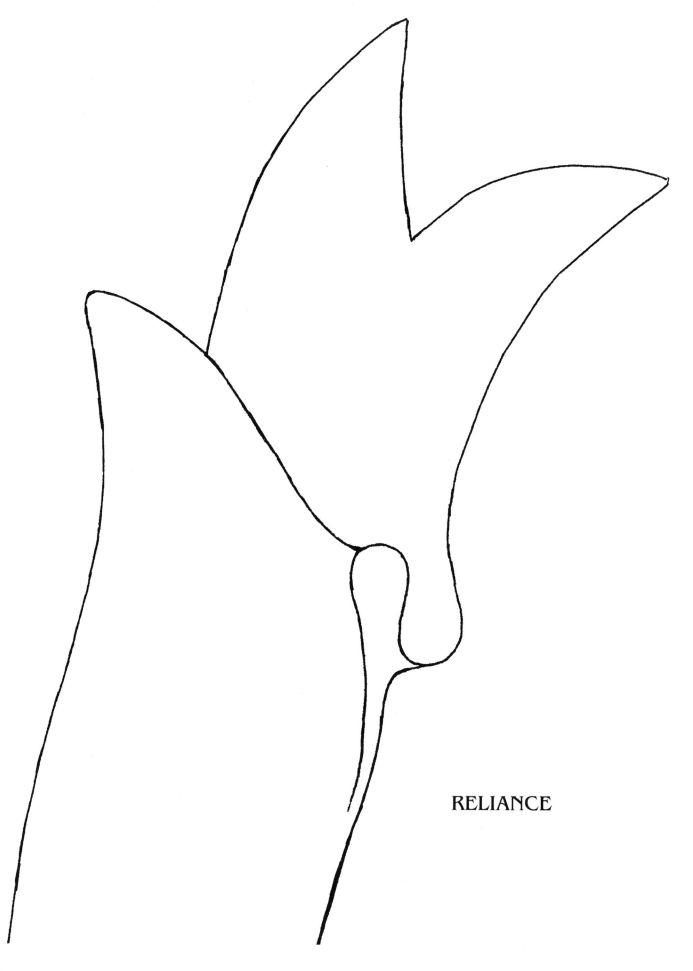

RELIANCE

DEFENDER

ENLARGE 110% FOR FULL SIZE

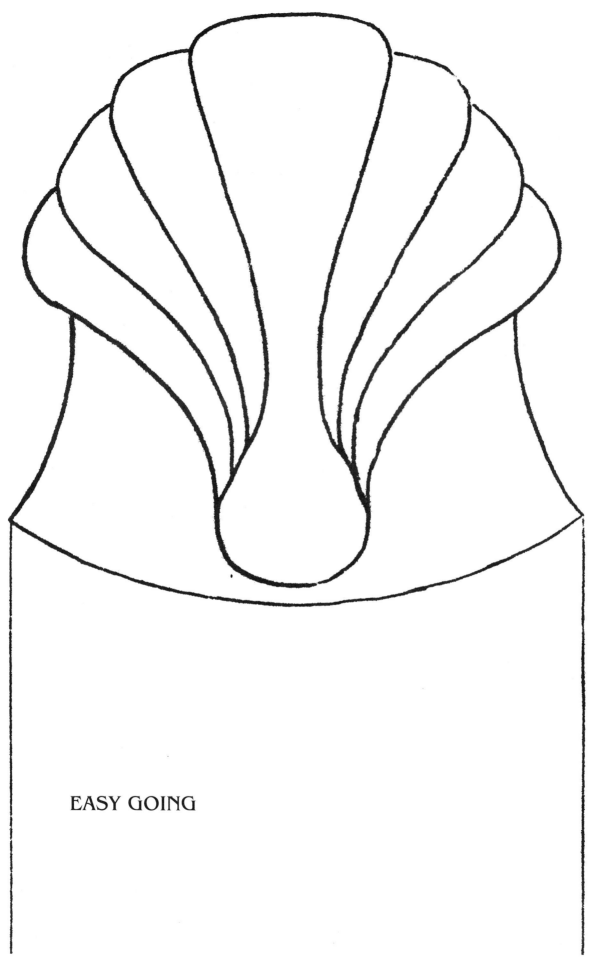

EASY GOING

PURITAN

ENLARGE 110%
FOR FULL SIZE

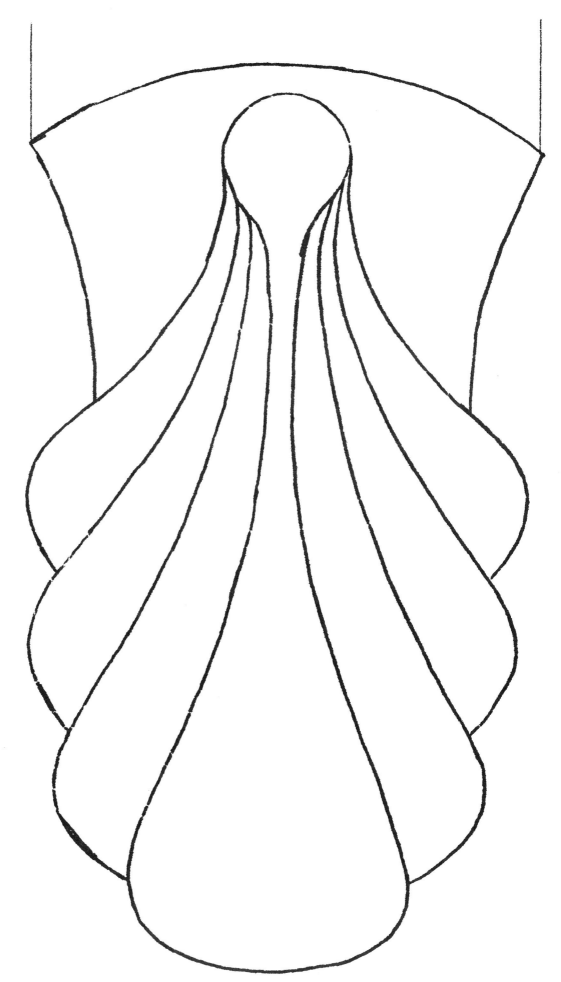

COLUMBIA

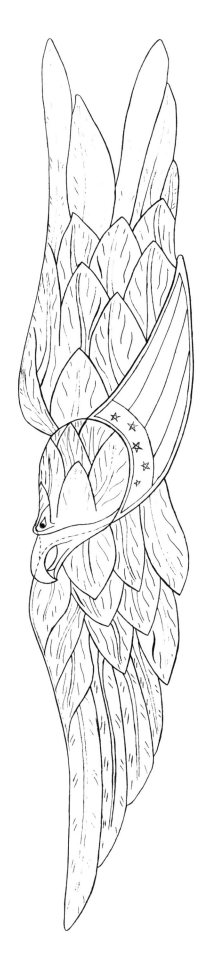

JAKE'S EAGLE & BELLAMY EAGLE SEE FOLD-OUT PAGES FOR LARGE VERSIONS

EAGLE AND SHIELD WITH TWO RIBBONS

SEE FOLD-OUT PAGES FOR LARGE VERSION

ABOUT THE AUTHOR

David was raised in Bellport, a small town on the south shore of Long Island. He learned his love of woodcarving there and his fascination with boats on Great South Bay.

He now resides in Cape Coral, Florida, with his wife Lyn and their 4-year-old son Jake. His daughters, Courtney and Lindsay, are leading successful lives in Westchester County, New York.

His first experience with producing a book was in the 1970s when he was Marine Carpentry Consultant for the Time-Life book, "THe Handy Boatman." Books of his to look forward to in the future include a story about his adventure as a deckboy on a Danish tramp steamer in 1964 and fully illustrated books on making decorative boat models and handcarved weathervanes.

When he is not carving he enjoys fly fishing and golf. In his career, he has carved over 5000 signs for customers in 28 states and 14 countries.

CRUISING SAILBOAT KINETICS
THE ART, SCIENCE & MAGIC OF
CRUISING BOAT DESIGN
by Danny Greene.
8½"x11", softcover, 256 pgs., photos & illustrations.

The classic book about boat design written for the everyday, non-professional sailor. **Cruising Sailboat Kinetics** demystifies boat design terminology and concepts. It opens up for recreational sailors a new world of understanding why sailboats act the way they do. It explains how boat designers transform sailing dreams and abstract design criteria into today's sleek, functional three-dimensional craft. Includes plans of some the best yacht designs of the last twenty years.

SEAWORTHINESS *THE FORGOTTEN FACTOR*
by C.A. Marchaj
7¾"x10½", hardcover, 384 pgs. with 140 line drawings & 50 photos.

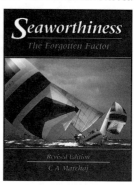

Newly updated and revised, this is a highly readable critical analysis of how the search for racing yacht performance has led to the development of sailing yachts with potentially dangerous seakeeping characteristics. Based upon the highest degree of practical and academic research, it demonstrates how modern yacht design often sacrifices safety for speed and for other considerations, and maintains that dramatic changes in design philosophy are needed to prevent further loss of life at sea. A major work which will help change popular design trends for both racing and cruising yachts. *"For the first time we are offered logical scientific criteria which help us to assess the likely seaworthiness of one boat or another. That is the great advance displayed in this book."* **Practical Boat Owner**

OF YACHTS & MEN
by William Atkin
8½"x11", softcover, 160 pgs., many photos, boat plans & illustrations.

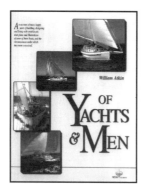

The famed boat designer's warm, entertaining and informative reminiscences of a lifetime enjoying boats. In his own words, it is *"an account of many happy years of building, designing and living with small boats; with plans and illustrations of some of these boats, and the circumstances under which they were conceived."* *"Whether you read purely for pleasure, or whether you want to feel, when the last page is turned, that you've been chatting informally with one who freely passes along nuggets of nautical lore from an infinite store, you can't afford to be without this book."* **Motor Boating Magazine**

THE GALLEY COLLECTION
VITTLES & DRINKS FOR ALL BOATS
by Ann Wilson, illustrated by JoGabeler Brooks
Softcover, 6"x9", 160 pages, illustrations.

Before casting off, someone must decide what to take for "vittles and drinks". **The Galley Collection** offers tried and true recipes to enhance the nautical experience as well as pracitical tips on creating menus, makings litst, outfitting the galley and provisioning. Recipes for all boats? Yes. Everything from a small ice chest to all-out soup-to-nuts. Only the participants know who has more fun. Cooking is a creative art, with plenty of latitude for experimenting and substtuting. **The Galley Collection** is your guide to good meals. What better place to enjoy them than on a boat?

TRUMPY
by Robert Tolf
Illustrated by Robert Picardat
11"x8½", hardcover, 224 pgs, 32 color plates, b&w photos & line drawings.

Trumpy celebrates the master craftsmanship and design represented by the renowned Trumpy yachts. John Trumpy designed and built the finest of yachts, both at Mathis Yacht Building Co. and at John Trumpy & Sons, Inc. **Trumpy's** many color illustrations and pen & ink sketches bring the boats to life. Includes original Trumpy plans, a complete list of all Trumpy yachts built and those known to survive. *"To honor the Trumpy legacy, Tiller Publishing of St. Michaels, MD, has produced its own masterpiece. . . . (Buy two books and cut one up for framing!)"* **Chesapeake Bay Magazine**

PRACTICAL JUNK RIG
DESIGN AERODYNAMICS AND HANDLING
by HG Hasler & JK McLeod
9¼" x11¼", hardcover, 244 pgs., color & b&w photos, tables & drawings.

In this encyclopedic volume the authors have synthesized 25 years of research and development of the junk rig. **Practical Junk Rig** examines the design and aerodynamic theory behind junk rigs and discusses how best to sail them. It examines the rig in detail, the principles that underlie it, considers possible alternative shapes and arrangements and performance. *"There is no better or more comprehensive work on the subject available . . . it should be considered THE handbook on junk rigs for anyone interested in the subject."* **Sailing**

BUILDING SWEET DREAM

AN ULTRALIGHT SOLO CANOE FOR
SINGLE & DOUBLE PADDLE
by Marc Pettingill
8½"x11", softcover, 176 pgs. illus.

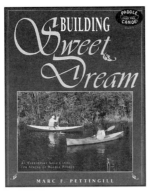

A complete how-to manual covering
all phases of building and finishing
12', 13' or 14' 28-lb. arc-bottom
canoes using "folded plywood" techniques. Includes dimensioned hull
plans, detailed building sequence
heavily illustrated with step-by-step photographs, and techniques
for painting and varnishing. *Sweet Dream* is easily and quickly
built using hand and basic electric tools, by one person in a one-
car garage or small workshop. ". . . .one of the loveliest canoes to
come out of a backyard. . . . ample photographs and diagrams, and the
instructional text is clear and un-ambiguous."
International Marine Boating Book Catalog, 1996

MARINE REINFORCED PLASTICS CONSTRUCTION

Manufacture & Repair
by John A. Wills
*Softcover, 8½"x11", 256
pages with many illustra-
tions and photographs.*

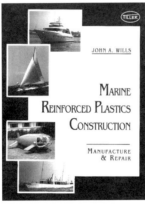

**Marine Reinforced
Plastics Construction**

takes a complex technical subject and distills the essence
into helpful, comprehensive and even entertaining terms.
Author John Wills introduces the reader to the subject of
marine reinforced plastics (what most of us refer to collec-
tively as "fiberglass"), offers solutions to blistering and
other problems and then challenges the reader with recent
discoveries and less conventional processes. One can opt
for a thorough grounding in the subject of plastics, the
solution to a pressing repair problem, or explore a new dis-
covery in marine plastics construction. John Wills freely
admits to being a "plastics-ophile" and provides a consum-
mate authority on the subject as well as a good read. "*This
is a highly authoritative overview of the materials and techniques used to
build the boats we call fiberglass. . . . From the outset, it is clear that
Wills is a plastics man . . . He loves the stuff, affectionately recalling how
his 'first whiff of acrylic monomer . . . smelled like a good martini.' . . .
Who should read this book? . . . any boatbuilder or yard man who is interested in making better boats and repairing them properly, as well as
boatowners with a technical interest in the subject of laminates, especially
those with a bad case of the pox.*" **Dan Spurr, Practical Sailor**

BUILDING THE WEEKEND SKIFF

by Richard Butz & John Montague
8½"x11", softcover, 180 pgs, many drawings & photos.

Contains scale plans, specifications,
tool list, well-illustrated step-by-
step-instructions for building a
handsome 15-foot rowing skiff.
Includes variations for sail and out-
board motor. By the authors of
Building the Six-Hour Canoe.

BUILDING THE SIX-HOUR CANOE

Design by Mike O'Brien
Text by Richard Butz
Illustrations by John Montague
Line Art by William Bartoo
8½"x11", softcover, 64 pgs. many photos & drawings.

Quickly and simply built, the Six-Hour Canoe is suitable for builders
and paddlers young and old . This book contains scale plans, specifications, a tool list, step-by-step instructions. All building operations
are illustrated with sketches and photographs. "*It's a great how-to, a
great read and probably will get as many folks into the wonderful world of
modest watercraft as the popular 'Instant Boat' series.*" **Messing About
in BOATS**

STEEL BOATBUILDING

FROM PLANS TO LAUNCHING
by Thomas Colvin
7"x10", softcover, 480 pgs., many illus.

This book combines both volumes of
Colvin's masterwork on building boats
from steel in one complete volume. **Steel
Boatbuilding** gives an overall view of
the subject from raw materials to the finished vessel. The wealth of detail perti-
nent to every step in the building, fitting out, and launching
of a 25- to 79-foot yacht or commercial vessel will ease the
first-time builder or the professional over problems that
might otherwise have seemed insurmountable. "*There is probably no one more uniquely qualified to pen the ultimate book on
steel boatbuilding than author, designer, builder and live-aboard
cruising man Tom Colvin.*" **Cruising World**

POCKET CRUISERS & TABLOID YACHTS, VOL. 1

Benford Design Group
8½"x11", softcover, 96 pgs., illus.
Complete building plans for several small cruising boats, including 14' and 20' tug yachts, 17' & 25' fantail steam launches, a 14' offshore cruising sloop and 20' catboat.
"All of the plans exhibit the professional presentation and well-conceived accommodations typical of the author's work." **WoodenBoat**

SMALL CRAFT PLANS

Benford Design Group
8½"x11", softcover, 96 pgs.
15 sets of plans for open boats, skiffs and tenders, from 7' to 18'. . *"Benford knows that readers will build directly from the book . . . In fact, he encourages the process by including full working drawings and tables of offsets for all of the designs."* **WoodenBoat**

CRUISING DESIGNS, FOURTH EDITION

Benford Design Group
8½"x11", softcover, 96 pgs, heavily illustrated with photos and line drawings.
A catalog of plans for great cruising boats, sail and power, for living aboard. The fourth edition includes a number of designs new since the third edition. *"His designs are like that: traditional but with contemporary elements, imaginative and unfettered by allegiance to rating rules or fashion, anachronistic, eclectic, eccentric, but always effective and user-friendly."* **Pacific Yachting**

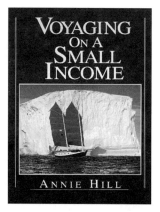

VOYAGING ON A SMALL INCOME

by Annie Hill
8½"x11", softcover, 192 pgs, photos, illustrations & drawings. Includes the Benford plywood and epoxy dory designs like the Hill's **Badger** and many variations from 26' to 37½'.
Annie and Peter Hill voyage on **Badger**, a Benford 34' Sailing Dory. An income of $3,000 per year lets them do this without worrying about stopping to work. They built **Badger** a decade ago, live aboard her, and have sailed her over 80,000 miles. Annie wrote this book to answer all the questions about what they're doing — a wealth of practical information on how-to-do-it is here. *"The best book we've read to date on liveaboard cruising."* **Messing About in BOATS**

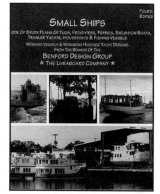

SMALL SHIPS, FOURTH EDITION

Benford Design Group
8½"x11", softcover, 304 pgs., color & b&w photos.

The latest volume of ideas from 'The Liveaboard Specialists,' it contains scores of detailed study plans of tugs, freighters, ferries, excursion boats, trawler yachts, houseboats and fishing vessels. *"Benford at his best . . . original, fun, and thought provoking, which is what makes this book worth owning, not just reading. It is a book which will be referred to again and again."* **Coastal Cruising**

NEW by Annie Hill — MANGOES & MUTTON

MANGOES & MUTTON is the long awaited and much anticipated second book by Annie Hill. For all those who have been entertained by Annie and Pete Hill's saga on **Badger,** the voyage continues. Now, **Badger** and her crew are off for the sailing adventure of a lifetime to Brazil and the Falkland Islands. In her typical, well-written fashion, Annie gives us enough technical niformation to satisfy any sailor as well as plenty of travel adventure to satisfy the sailor's soul. *Available in 1998.*